*Good and Bad Ways*

*to Think about*

*Religion*

*and Politics*

# Good and Bad Ways to Think about Religion and Politics

ROBERT BENNE

William B. Eerdmans Publishing Company

Grand Rapids, Michigan / Cambridge, U.K.

Published 2010 by

Wm. B. Eerdmans Publishing Co.

2140 Oak Industrial Drive N.E., Grand Rapids, Michigan 49505 /

P.O. Box 163, Cambridge CB3 9PU U.K.

Printed in the United States of America

16  15  14  13  12  11  10        7  6  5  4  3  2  1

**Library of Congress Cataloging-in-Publication Data**

Benne, Robert.

Good and bad ways to think about religion and politics / Robert Benne.

p.      cm.

ISBN 978-0-8028-6364-5 (pbk.: alk. paper)

1. Christianity and politics — United States.

2. Religion and politics.   I. Title.

BR516.B395    2010

261.7 — dc22

2010005671

www.eerdmans.com

*For my grandchildren —*
*Dylan, Linnea, Kai, Andrew,*
*Alex, Ian, and Max*

# Contents

*Chapter One*

# Introduction: Why Another Book on Religion and Politics?

Why in the world would one want to write another book on religion and politics? Any brief glance at the catalogue of a library or any quick search through an online search engine will bring forth a huge number of entries. Is there anything about the subject that hasn't been said?

It is certainly true that much has been said, but a good deal of what has been said is genuinely bad. There is nothing greater than indignation to stimulate a writer to write, and my outrage has been stirred mightily by reading so many wrongheaded "takes" on how religion and politics ought to be related. In this book I will describe and analyze the bad ways and then offer what I consider to be a better way.

I am so bold as to think that the Christian tradition from which I write — the Lutheran tradition — offers such a better way. It has an approach to faith and politics that has scarcely been heard in the larger public debate about the relation of religion and politics. Indeed, that way of looking at religion and politics is generally neglected even by the church that supposedly bears it. Moreover, though I prize that tradition and will be writing from it, the tradition itself needs some revision in order to

1

grapple creatively with the new challenges we face. I hope to offer that revision for the ongoing conversation.

My contribution will have to do mainly with how religious persons, institutions, and the religious claims they make *ought* to interact with the political process. I will argue with those who have very different versions of how religion and politics ought to be related, or in many cases, unrelated.

This normative task needs to be distinguished from the descriptive task of showing how religion in fact makes an impact on the political process. Both tasks are currently very important to both scholars and the general public in the contemporary world. The Pew Trust, for example, with its massive study of American religion, includes extensive information about how religious factors influence political behavior. And of course we have many examples of religious organizations and individuals trying to influence political decisions, some praiseworthy and others more dubious.

Oddly enough, neither the normative nor the descriptive tasks were considered to be very important fifty years ago. There would have been far fewer books on the subject then, and of course there were no computer search engines to look up the subject because there were few computers available to ordinary people. Even the computers would not have found much, except for the controversy in 1960 over John F. Kennedy's successful effort in becoming the first Catholic President. In the run-up to that election Kennedy assured alarmed Baptist pastors that not only would his church have no influence over his actions as President, but that his own religion — such as it was — would have no influence on his political decisions.

After that flurry the relative uninterest in the relation of religion and politics returned, though there were many examples of organized religion's effect on American political life. The major example of such effects came during the civil rights movement of the late 50s and the 60s. The black churches, aided by a number of white denominations, and led by a black Baptist preacher, Martin Luther King Jr., exerted great political pressure to get rid of racist laws and practices and to bestow long-denied civil rights to minority blacks. There was also religious involvement in the anti-war movement during the Vietnam War, as well as incursions into the newly born ecological, feminist, and gay rights movements. The Catholic and mainline Protestant denominations exerted political clout amid the political controversies of the day.

This religious involvement in politics was pretty much ignored in academia, as well as in the book-publishing world. In those elite worlds religion was no longer supposed to have political potency. Even the strong religious elements in the King-led civil rights movement were often ignored in the academic accounts of that phenomenon. Academics were long schooled in modernization theories that assumed that people would become less religious as living standards and the level of education rose. If religion was becoming weaker as America modernized, why bother studying something that was about to disappear?

Since most of the historians, sociologists, political scientists, and even scholars of religion of the time believed in and participated themselves in this "modernization" process, they were very unlikely to take the religious factor in political life seriously. Moreover, modernization theory was abetted by a related powerful intellectual perspective of the time, the Enlightenment paradigm, which held that only reason and science could arrive at reliable knowledge. The Enlightenment, partly in response to the wars of religion, viewed religion as arbitrary, unreliable, irrational, and therefore potentially oppressive if it were asserted in the public sphere. Therefore religion, if adhered to at all, *ought* to remain private and politically unimportant.

Intellectuals, then, were blinkered by two convictions — that religion was waning in the modernizing world and that whatever was left of it ought to remain private. In their eyes, religion did not and ought not have any discernible effect on politics. So they ignored it. This posture endured, with a few notable exceptions such as Peter Berger, until the recent past in academia. However, events made such obliviousness impossible.

First came the election of Jimmy Carter in 1976. Conservative evangelicals — scarcely known and much defiled — seemed to come out of the woodwork to elect a fellow evangelical. Little did those evangelicals know what they were getting at the time. Soon after the Carter election came the crisis in Iran, which signaled the rise of radical Islam. That resurgence became impossible to ignore, as it deeply affected the Muslim countries of the Middle East. Radical Islam was quintessentially political — it aimed at capturing the political centers of power and imposing Islamic law on the newly "pure" nations. It also aimed at dramatically extending the reach of Islam. Religion was becoming intensely political. The academic world belatedly began to take account of it.

What really got the wheels turning, however, was the rise of organized conservative religion in America. The Supreme Court decision of 1973 that found a constitutional right to abortion was an early stimulus to the rise of conservative Protestantism. The Court seemed to usurp the will of the people and to trample on religious values. Soon thereafter ensued an increasing number of court decisions that seemed to drive religious themes and practices out of public life. Meanwhile, the counterculture of the 60s worked its way into the fabric of American life in the 70s and 80s.

These developments galvanized conservative Protestantism into a political force through organizations such as the Moral Majority and later the Christian Coalition. These organizations gave increasing visibility to the awakening giant of American evangelicalism, which now constitutes the largest segment of

American religious groups at about 26 percent, according to a recent Pew study of American religion. The emergence of such a large group has stimulated the fears of many secular intellectuals, some of whom I will discuss later, who still cling to various versions of the modernization thesis or the Enlightenment paradigm. A few of them furrow their brows in fear of putative theocracy in America, something that is as likely as a snowball in hell.

Indeed, it is increasingly clear that American evangelicalism is neither religiously nor politically monolithic even though it is politically very active. A significant portion will vote Democratic while most ally themselves with the Republicans. But even conservative evangelicals have more nuanced perspectives on politics than they are given credit for. Conversely, the headquarters of the mainline Protestant denominations — Episcopal, Presbyterian, Methodist, United Church of Christ, and the Evangelical Lutheran Church in America — continue their political activism by listing further to the left than their lay membership. They remain very active politically but with few followers among their own laity.

American Catholicism, while holding its "market share" among the religions of America because of Latino immigration, attempts with more effect to influence American political life. It draws upon the Pope's moral authority and an ample store of social teachings to make its arguments. But it has been badly damaged by the fallout from sexual abuse by its priests. Its moral clout has been diminished. African American churches, in contrast to the examples of Jeremiah Wright and Al Sharpton, tend to be less active politically as institutions even as their members remain staunchly Democratic in political orientation. Reform Judaism has become more and more identified with the political causes of liberal Protestantism (except for the latter's stance on Israel), while Orthodox and Conservative organizations are more diffident about politics.

So, it seems that religion is relevant to politics in an empirical sense. And many persons — pundits and academics among them — now reflect and write profusely upon this lively connection. The question is not so much whether American religion will have political effects. It most definitely will. The more serious questions are: Should it? How should it? Certainly some modes of religious involvement are harmful to both the religious organizations and society. But perhaps the worst damage is done to religion itself. It is used as an instrument for purposes other than its own main reason for being. It sacrifices its transcendent claims for a mess of earthly pottage.

Chapters Two and Three of this book will feature an analysis of the two main bad ways of relating religion and politics — one in which religion and politics are separated and the other in which they are fused. Both bad ways break down into subcategories. The fourth chapter will deal with the theory of how religion and politics ought to be related, what I call "critical engagement." How do the core claims of religion properly relate to something as specific as voting for a candidate or for a specific public policy? The fifth chapter will deal with the practical ways that religion does and ought to relate to political life. I will develop a typology of involvement that runs from non-controversial and subtle ways to controversial and robustly assertive, and will make evaluative comments as I survey the types.

*Chapter Two*

# The Separationists

## A. "To Keep Politics Free of Dangerous Religion"

The first bad way to think about religion and politics is sharply to separate them, claiming that they should have nothing to do with each other, either theoretically or practically. This separationism comes from both militant secularists and ardent religious people, and in both crude and sophisticated forms. But it also pops up in a camp that could be termed "selective separationists," who believe that only certain kinds of religion should be banned from politics. Thus, they are not true separationists. We shall reflect about them toward the end of this first section.

During a recent political discussion on our campus, one of our physics professors, a devoted reader of *The Nation,* angrily denounced those Christian groups who are active in pressing for policies that restrain abortion. Finding ridiculous the belief that a clump of cells is viewed as the beginning of life by these activists, he makes the following statement:

> We live in a free society so it's fine for people to believe this
> very simplistic philosophical principle (that life begins at

conception), to incorporate it into dogma for their religious practice, and to freely meet with others of the same belief. But it is dead wrong to expect others to drink from such thin philosophical soup and to attempt to legislate public policy into this mode.

And from the right, the redoubtable George Will condemns those local groups of Christian social conservatives who try to make some room for Intelligent Design in high school science curricula. Will quotes the famous saying of Thomas Jefferson that "It does me no injury for my neighbor to say there are twenty gods, or no god. It neither picks my pocket nor breaks my leg." However, if such religious opinions become public, Mr. Jefferson made quite a different judgment. George Will has the same negative opinion of such religion becoming public: "It is injurious, and unneighborly, when zealots try to compel public education to infuse theism into scientific education."[1]

Many other persons and groups make similar assessments of the public exercise of religion through churches, voluntary associations, or even individual persons. Often, in their distaste for religion becoming public, they confuse the "separation of church and state" with "the interaction of religion and politics," which is quite a different matter. The former prohibits the state from establishing or privileging particular religious organizations and the persons belonging to them, a thoroughly institutional matter. The latter is guaranteed by the First Amendment, which protects the "free exercise of religion" by persons and organizations. Free exercise certainly isn't limited to the private sphere. But for those worried about the threats posed by dangerous religion, perhaps such a distinction doesn't matter. They seem to be willing to refuse freedom of expression to people and

1. George Will, *Roanoke Times*, November 20, 2005.

organizations if they operate from religious ideas and values, a somewhat shocking proposal.

Militant atheists such as Richard Dawkins *(The God Delusion)* do not shrink from such a proposal. Dawkins is so negative toward religion — it seems to him to be the source of all the world's woes — that he suggests that teaching religion to young children is a form of child abuse. Joined by other popular atheist authors — Sam Harris, Christopher Hitchens, Daniel Dennett — Dawkins no doubt believes that irrational and dangerous religion ought to remain safely sequestered from politics. To them the "separation of church and state" would also include the separation of religion from politics.

A more sophisticated version of this separationism is offered by Mark Lilla in his influential book, *The Stillborn God,* in which he argues that religion that appears in public inevitably becomes "political theology," a very bad thing indeed. Political theology, if it actually becomes influential, will lead toward theocracy. Lilla fears that the vigor of conservative religion in the United States is in danger of undermining a fragile, liberal democracy. Thus, he much prefers that religion remain separate from politics in America. He is joined by authors such as Damon Linker, whose *Theocons: Secular America Under Siege,* worries that a cabal of conservative Catholic intellectuals is plotting to take over American political life.

While Lilla and Linker are not as hostile to religion *per se* as the Dawkins crowd, they do believe that intense religion is dangerous. If people hold their religion lightly and with sufficient skepticism, it does not become dangerous because it will not have enough energy to carry it into the public sphere. Many academics hold this point of view.

Closely related to this sophisticated separationism is another variety that holds that expressing religiously based moral values in political life is a violation of the liberal settlement that has kept political life free and tolerant. They too equate the principle of separation of church and state with the separation of religion and politics. These separatists — the ACLU, Americans for Separation of Church and State, and a number of secular political philosophers come to mind — believe that the Founders were classical liberals who meant for only secular, "public" reason to guide the political sphere. Religious convictions were by their own nature so parochial, irrational, numerous, and arbitrary that they ought to remain private where they could do no harm. What's more, such convictions are claimed by religious actors to be anchored in ultimate truth, which invests them with undue certainty in the minds of the activists. Thus, for these separationists the fact that some political proposal or conviction arises from religious grounds is enough to rule it out of public discourse. Only rational, universal, secular moral arguments ought to be exercised in political life.

So we have a number of perspectives contending that religion and religiously based morality ought to be kept out of political life. They much prefer a *Naked Public Square,* the phrase Richard Neuhaus coined as his description of a public life sealed off from religious presence and action.

Such an interpretation of liberalism moves toward what could be called "liberal totalitarianism," in which a single standard of what counts as reason and a single vocabulary of political discussion are enforced. Of course, that standard and vocabulary are the property of the secular elite, who then enjoy an enormous advantage in public life. When policy is then shaped under those conditions it is imposed on all sectors of society, including civil society and the family. Religious life then has to bend to the dictates of such liberal policies. (We see this already happening in the effort to enforce anti-discrimination policies — especially those having to do with homosexual orientation and conduct — against traditional religious and civic groups whose own internal principles prohibit such behavior.) Here we have an example of public, political principles invading the religious sphere rather than vice versa.

Truth be told, most of these objections to the role of religion in political life amount to what I earlier termed "selective separationism." What they are concerned about is the influence of politically active *conservative* religion, which they often call "fundamentalism." They then lump it together with other fundamentalisms, including radical Islam. They believe that such religion should be barred or at least marginalized from political life. Conservative religion resists "progressive" causes that they support, or it agitates for causes that they consider to be retrograde or downright wrong. Conservative religion of a Catholic, Protestant, or Jewish sort tends to resist stem cell research, the redefining of marriage and the family, the neo-Darwinism taught in the public schools, the sexualization of popular culture, the separation of law from its moral and religious foundations, an activist judiciary that overrules democratic political decisions, and a general permissiveness in the culture. On the other hand, conservative religious organizations and persons are likely to support the war in Iraq/Afghanistan, strong defense at home and democratization abroad, a free space for religious belief and practice, the death penalty, abstinence-oriented sex education, and increased restriction of abortion.

"Selective separationists" are so bothered by conservative religion's influence that they seem blind to the ongoing role of liberal religion's efforts in political life. It is the so-called "Religious Right" that they are really alarmed about. When the militant atheists and the proponents of a naked public square rail against public religion, it is almost always religion of a conservative sort. They seem to assume that only the policies supported by conservative religion are coercive, when in fact all policies that become law are coercive, including those supported by "progressive" religion and "secular reason." Laws that prohibit sexual and racial discrimination are just as coercive as those that restrain the practice of abortion, for example, that prohibit "partial-birth" abortion. Any policy that becomes law has the force of the state behind it and is implicitly or explicitly coercive.

Some selective separationists are clear and upfront about their target. Andrew Sullivan, who himself claims to be a conservative, targets the Religious Right as the toxic element corrupting true conservatism. In his *The Conservative Soul: Fundamentalism, Freedom, and the Future of the Right,* Sullivan argues that "fundamentalism," in which he includes all religious conservatives, even the Pope, amounts to a rejection of reason. As a person who also purports to be a Catholic, Sullivan might be thought to respect the social teachings of his church, but those too seem to fall under his categorical denunciation of "fundamentalism." In other words, if religious conservatives hold political opinions that conflict with Sullivan's brand of conservatism, they are irrational. They should be thoroughly purged from modern-day conservatism and marginalized from political life in general. He holds no such animus against religious activists of a progressive sort, even though he claims conservative sympathies.

Others are milder in their worries about the political muscle of religious conservatives. Writers such as Kathleen Kennedy Townsend call for more balance in religion's impact on the political realm. Although her book, *Failing America's Faithful: How Today's Churches Are Mixing God with Politics and Losing Their Way,* sounds like a denunciation of the interaction of religion and politics in general, it is not really that. Rather, she calls liberal Christians to renew their moral commitment to social justice through politics and at the same time defeat the retrograde conservatives who push their pet causes — such as the decrease of abortion — onto an unwary world. Only some kinds of religion should be politically active.

In his *Faith and Politics: How the "Moral Values" Debate Divides America and How to Move Forward Together*, former Senator John Danforth decries the passion injected into political life by religion of both the left and right. But the "moral values" debate, which he laments, is actually focused on issues that religious conservatives really care about — cultural issues such as end-of-life procedures, stem cell research, and abortion. These, he believes, should be withdrawn from public debate, along with the religious conservatives who care about them.

In short, we have many books lamenting the incursion of religion in politics, but on closer look they express worry mainly about conservative religion's impact on politics. Conservative religion is the "dangerous religion" that concerns them. They — even the despisers of religion in general — have little to say about liberal Christianity's political support for "progressive" candidates, policies, and causes. Few of them protest Protestant Liberalism's advocacy efforts in political life for the causes they approve of — criticism of the Bush administration and its policies, especially its Middle East policies. The reason for this interesting oversight is that "progressive religion" is so accommodated to liberal, elite culture that it is difficult to see where one ends and the other begins.

Nevertheless, we have to deal with the argument that religion and politics should be kept completely separate, even if most of the arguments are disingenuous in that they are alarmed at only some kinds of religious involvement in politics.

To this separationist argument we have several rejoinders: constitutional, historical, practical, and theological. In the first place, the Founders determined that the free exercise of religion was not only to be protected in the Bill of Rights; such exercise was to them the "first freedom." They recognized that true religion could not be coerced, so they guaranteed freedom of religious association and belief. Such religion, they believed, would be more vital and creative than the established religions that they knew firsthand from experience with established churches. Thus, they prohibited the establishment of a particular church at the national level. But they also knew that serious religion would necessarily issue in conduct of both a private and public sort. Indeed, they prized the importance of religion in shaping a virtuous citizenry. Further, they knew that persons and organizations holding serious religious convictions would naturally impact public life with their notions of what is good, right, and just, as well as with their own self-interest. The free exercise clause meant that religiously grounded morality could rightfully find its way into political life. The more intemperate of the separationists seem to be willing to abrogate this "first freedom," especially with regard to religious conservatives. Fortunately, American courts will most likely resist the curtailment of the free exercise of religion, which has allowed — even encouraged — the exercise of religiously based morality.

Such free exercise certainly has been a historical reality in America. The American Revolution itself was fueled in part by fervor set off by the Great Awakening, a religious movement of the first order. Religious organizations and persons were deeply involved in Abolition, in Prohibition, and more recently in the Civil Rights Act of 1964. They have been active and influential in many public issues in the nation's history. And they continue to affect policy, sometimes in a major way (the ending of Apartheid, legislating restraints on abortion) but more generally in smaller and less visible ways. The Pew Forum on Religion has found, for instance, that intensity of religious belief is perhaps the most important ingredient in voting patterns. The more frequently persons worship the more likely they are to be conservative politically.

This vast and complicated interplay of religion and public life in America simply cannot be shut down. It is impractical, indeed, impossible, to shut off such interaction if we continue to prize civil liberties and religious freedom in this country. How could one practically prohibit churches and pastors from discussing public issues and making their opinions known about such issues? Even the totalitarian states generated by Communism and Fascism could not shut off such discussion though they tried very hard to do so. And, of course, America's commitment to religious freedom is so ingrained in public and private life that such curtailment is unthinkable. Even more impractical is the notion that the state or society could prevent individual persons from acting on their innermost religious convictions. That would be impossible even under the strictest sort of totalitarianism. Short of some sort of thought control, persons cannot be prevented from holding private religious convictions and exercising them in covert ways in the public sphere. Even if they do not overtly state or express them, they still can hold them and act on them.

Finally, there are important theological reasons why religion cannot be separated from politics. The dominant American religions — Judaism and mainstream Christianity — insist that the God they worship and to whose will they strive to conform is a God of the whole world, not just a God of the inner reaches of the human heart. God is sovereign over creation and history. Worshipers of such a God pledge themselves to follow his will in their private and public lives, though admittedly it may be more complicated to do so in public life. Serious practitioners of these religions are obligated to do the right or the good in all of life, not just private life. Thus, they seek political parties and policies that they believe are most continuous with their own self-interest and conceptions of right, good, and just, and that are also practical and feasible. Asking them to drop their religious convictions as they enter into public life is asking them to ignore the source of their moral principles. Serious religion inevitably has a public dimension.

On the other hand, in response to those who worry about the theocratic possibilities of religion precisely because of its public dimension, we offer the following reflections. The first is historical in nature. Christians are quite aware that those episodes in Christianity's long history in the West in which it tried to wield political power violated one of its essential principles — that the church is given only the persuasive power of the Word, not the coercive power of the sword. One of the major criticisms of medieval Catholicism by the Reformers was that the church had involved itself too directly in worldly politics. It had confused its God-given mission of the gospel with the worldly task of politics and had thereby corrupted its sacred calling.

The propensity to become too identified with worldly power also involved the churches in the Wars of Religion, which, even though not primarily religious in nature, continue to be a terrible stain upon those who claimed to follow the One who prayed for the unity of all his followers. This memory makes the vast majority of Christians reluctant to claim for the church any direct political power. Even the most activist Christians abhor a return to a Christendom in which the church wields political power. While religious persons and organizations want to influence politics, it is a huge stretch to claim that they want exclusive and direct power over it.

There is a more profound theological reason why theocracy does not provide an attractive option for classical Christians. All three classical Christian traditions — the Catholic, the Lutheran, and the Reformed — have theologies that clearly differentiate between the church's mission, its guiding principles, and the means of furthering them, on the one hand, and the state's purposes, guiding principles, and means of realizing them, on the other. All three recognize a tentative dualism between the church and the world, though both are under the sovereign will of God and cannot finally be separated.

The church and its participants live amid two different ways that God reigns, one in which he rules through the gospel and one in which he rules through civil authorities. Believers voluntarily assent to the rule of the gospel in their lives, while the same believers — and non-believers alike — are governed with or without their assent by the coercive law of civil authorities, whose laws are backed up by the threat of force. The gospel's content is given by the Bible and sacred tradition; the civil sphere's laws and practices are shaped by a mixture of tradition (including religious tradition), reason, natural law, and human experience. When Christians hold authority in the civil realm, they are subject to the guidance of that realm and its principles, though they bring their particular Christian outlook to bear on that realm. But there is no simple importation of the claims of the gospel and the church into the world, nor is there a simple importation of the claims of the world into the realm of the gospel and the church. Both have their own integrity but not ultimate autonomy; both are under the rule of God, but in very different ways.

Thus, there are good theological reasons why classical Christians do not desire theocracy. Neither the church — nor individual Christians *qua* Christians — are given the mandate by God to govern the world. Yet, the church and individual Christians want to be able to exercise their intellectual and moral beliefs in the public, political sphere. They want the right to participate vigorously in the public realm according to their own deepest beliefs, just like all other citizens. They rightly want participation, not control. The separationists who believe that religion presents a high danger to politics — few though they really are — are wrong in their thinking about the relation of religion and politics in American life.

We must admit, however, that some religious organizations and individual Christians sometimes draw too tight a connection between their central religious convictions and particular public policies. But the danger in those cases is not so much to our democracy as it is to the integrity of the faith that they are promoting. Our democracy and our society are far too permeated by checks and balances for religious groups to work their will dangerously. But making too tight connections can lead to another bad way to think about religion and politics — when both are fused together. We will deal with that issue in the next chapter.

### B. "To Keep Religion Free of Dangerous Politics"

While one kind of separationism tries to keep religion and politics completely separate because of its fear that religion is destructive of politics, there is another kind that separates religion from politics because of the danger political involvement has for authentic religion. This second kind of separationism — though admirable and understandable in many cases — is also a bad way to think about the relation of religion and politics.

There is a praiseworthy — even noble — motive behind some of this second kind of separationism. Classical Christians believe that the gospel is transcendent in several ways. First, it comes from God and breaks into our fallen world. The coming of Christ is not our doing. So anything that we do — politics, for instance — cannot be identified with the gospel of Christ. Second, those repentant souls who accept the gospel are not saved because of their membership and activity in any political group. The gospel transcends such worldly divisions. Christians fall into many political beliefs and parties but yet are open to and grasped by the gospel. There may be limits for Christians as to what political activities they might legitimately participate in, but for the most part, their membership in the Body of Christ transcends political divisions. Finally, the gospel makes claims

18

about ultimacy — what is finally true about life, while politics of a democratic sort claims to represent the very worldly voice of the people, which certainly does not claim ultimacy.

Therefore, identifying the gospel with any worldly political program or using the gospel for political purposes subverts the very nature of the gospel. This second sort of separationism certainly protects the gospel from these kinds of depredation.

What sorts of separationism, then, are we talking about, and what is wrong with them? We'll start with classical sectarianism and then move through other types of religious separationism.

Classical sectarians believe that the gospel and the church it gathers ought to be untainted by the fallenness of the world. They are surprisingly optimistic about the church and thoroughly pessimistic about the world. Taking their cues from the New Testament letters of John, sectarians see themselves and their churches as besieged enclaves in a world gone to hell. Their churches, they believe, can maintain high standards of belief and conduct only if they separate from the world, especially from politics. They aim at a true believer's church.

Sectarians invariably take the pacifistic elements of the Sermon on the Mount as the key to Christian belief and life. Turning the other cheek, forgiving seventy times seven, offering the robber all that one has, not resisting violence aimed at the self — all of these become central principles for the Christian life. On the other hand, they see the world as full of violence. Politics itself is based on coercion — people are coerced by laws enacted by the state. And those laws are backed up by the threat and actuality of violence if they are disobeyed. The world is thoroughly contaminated by coercion and violence. There is no compromise — one must either be a Christian devoted to peace or participate in a violence-drenched public world. One cannot serve God and mammon.

Sectarianism, a minority strand in Christian history, continues to flourish in many Mennonite traditions, running from the Old Order Amish to the more accommodated Church of the Brethren. But all shun participation in the police and military, which would involve blatant violations of their own key principles. Further, the Amish refuse to participate in politics, which involves coercion as well as accommodation to other features of the modern world. Even Mennonites and Church of the Brethren members are unlikely to be found in electoral politics. Participation in politics is dangerous to true religious practice.

There is a newer version of sectarianism represented by Stanley Hauerwas and his followers. This is sectarianism with a difference. Instead of withdrawing from the public world, these sectarians make vigorous efforts to expose the world for what it is — a radically fallen world based on coercion and finally on violence. They do this by exemplifying in their own personal and church lives a commitment to non-violence and peace, which they believe is the center of Jesus' teaching. They refuse to participate in military or police action, and are reluctant to participate personally in formal politics. One of their main purposes in all this is to point out how deeply the world is enmeshed in coercion and violence, and to witness to another way, the "politics of Jesus."

Such principled pacifism is praiseworthy in many ways, but it has huge theological and ethical problems that disbar it from being a good way to think about the relation of religion and politics. For some sectarians, it seems as if creation and history are no longer under the sovereign will of God, but have rather been turned over to Satan. God has withdrawn from the ordinary world, and evil powers hold sway. Therefore, Christians must retreat into enclaves to await the time when God will put an end to this God-forsaken world.

But this leaves God the Father — Creator, Sustainer, Judge — out of the picture and thereby violates the First Article of the Apostles' and Nicene Creeds. All classical Christian traditions hold that God is actively involved in and sovereign over the world and its history. There may be a struggle going on between God and Satan, but the world is contested territory, not one in which Satan has dominion. Christians cannot give up on the world; they must actively participate in God's care for the world, even if that means involvement in coercive activities such as politics.

Other sorts of sectarians may indeed believe in the sovereignty of God, but they believe Christians must not participate in coercive means to cooperate with God in his maintenance of the world. Christians are called to suffer when the winds of history blow against them. They are not even to use coercive or violent means to protect their neighbor. The sovereign God in due time will execute fair judgment, if not in this life then in another. To this claim classical Christians maintain that Christians can and should participate in God's governance even if that means the use of coercion and violence. Luther, for example, wrote treatises defending the moral legitimacy of the military life, and even that of a hangman. Jesus' injunctions against violence do not apply to social and political life in this age. These classical traditions hold to principles that allow the justified use of coercion and violence, sometimes called "just war theory." They believe that Christians can rightfully participate in military action (if it is justified), police work, and certainly politics. In fact, they have an obligation to participate in politics, and through politics in military and police actions. Further, they are called to employ their Christian religious resources in their interaction with politics. Religion indeed connects with politics because we ought to be responsible participants with God in serving the neighbor by preserving a just order on earth.

There are other theological arguments that seem, like some sectarian perspectives, to separate the order of creation (totally fallen) from the order of redemption (the gospel). For example, in Lutheran theology there is the danger of allowing worldly orders (politics being one of them) to become autonomous from religiously grounded moral and intellectual values. This approach refuses to allow those values to offer critique and guidance to politics. It assumes that politics is driven by principles totally different than those of Christian ethics. The gospel is made so transcendent that it does not engage the world, especially politics.

For example, a Lutheran theologian of the nineteenth century, Christian Luthardt, argued that "The Gospel has absolutely nothing to do with outward existence but only with eternal life. . . . It is not the vocation of Jesus Christ or of the Gospel to change the orders of secular life and establish them anew. . . . Christianity wants to change man's heart, not his external situation."[2] There are two serious theological problems here. For one, the affirmation of the sovereign God as Creator, Sustainer, and Judge of all is forgotten. The God whose will is revealed in the commandments and in his involvement in history is somehow expunged from the political world. Along with this denial of God's involvement in history is an elevation of the gospel to such a height that it has no relevance to ordinary life. The gospel addresses only the inner man about eternal life, not the whole man who is embedded in God's history.

On the contrary, Christians as individuals and members of churches properly bring to bear the whole Trinitarian faith on our involvement in the world. While there is no simple application of that faith to the world, there is deep theological warrant for keeping faith and world in a lively relationship. Such a tendency to denude the faith of worldly relevance is replayed by those in Christian higher education who argue that classrooms in Christian colleges should look pretty much like those in good

2. Quoted in Carl Braaten, *Principles of Lutheran Theology* (Minneapolis: Augsburg Fortress, 2007), p. 124.

secular schools. Learning is given over to the guidance of science, reason, and historical experience. The faith in its full Trinitarian form has no relevance to claims made from those secular sources.

But such a separation between faith and learning is analogous to the separation of the claims of the faith from those of politics. Neither kind adequately accounts for God's involvement in all of human affairs, the fact of the fallenness of both secular truth-claims and politics, or the relevance of Christian faith-claims for the world. The historical effects of such deficiencies have been very serious. The separation of classical Christian faith from politics paved the way in Germany for passivity of Christians before the rise of the Nazi movement. Similar political passivity occurred in the struggle over Apartheid in South Africa. Passivity in the world of education has led to a widespread secularization of Christian higher education by disallowing the challenges that Christian claims can and should make in the classroom.

The vast majority of separationism, however, is not driven by faulty theology. Most is a product of practical tendencies to separate religion from ordinary life — Sunday from Monday through Saturday. People don't have to be sectarians or dualists in theory; they just think and act in ways that separate religion and ordinary life, including politics. One major reason for such dualism is that since the coming of modern times in the eighteenth century, each sector of life is increasingly divided from other sectors of life, each being purportedly guided by its own autonomous principles. So practical wisdom gives the verdict that "religion and politics don't mix." Religion and science don't mix. Religion and business don't mix. Religion and art don't mix. Religion and sport don't mix. So Christians segment themselves according to the sector of life that they inhabit at the time. They are bifurcated or trifurcated Christians.

While there is some truth to this segmentation — there is a tentative autonomy to these various sectors — there is no final autonomy. From a Christian point of view all sectors are under the sovereignty of God, and he is active in them. The Christian is called to make sense of them from both a worldly and a Christian point of view, and to act as best as possible in them according to the will of God. There can be no areas that are free and clear from the presence and commands of God. Practical separationism is as bad as theoretical separationism. Both must be rejected by serious, classical Christians. They lead to bad ways of thinking about religion and politics. Neither the separationism that fears religion's involvement in politics nor the separationism that fears politics' contamination of religion is compelling. However, before we take up the way that religion and politics ought to be related, we need to examine another bad way to think about religion and politics. It is to that task that we turn.

*Chapter Three*

# The Fusionists

## A. The Political Use of Religion

A very bad way to think of the relation of religion and politics is to bring them so close together they actually meld together. They become fused. This is just as destructive to true Christianity as to separate completely Christian claims from politics. Fusing creates politicized religion or religionized politics, a disaster for both religion and politics. Politicized religion reduces religious claims to this-worldly dynamics. Instead of salvation for all, politicized religion offers salvation only to those on the right side of political fault lines. Instead of salvation freely offered by God in Christ, politicized religion offers salvation to those who work for particular political causes. Instead of salvation freely offered and received, politicized religion often entails coercion to accept its claims. On the other hand, religionized politics elevates what should be this-worldly claims to ultimate status. Politics gets raised beyond its reach and often stretches toward messianic proportions. Indeed, the twentieth century found two messianic political movements that claimed far more lives than any religious crusade ever did. Both Nazism and Communism, quasi-religious movements, claimed to bring a utopian conclusion to history. The Nazis aimed at bringing a Thousand Year Kingdom while the Communists aimed at bringing about a stateless utopia. Both operated with the force of religious passion behind them, even though both were murderously committed to destroying Christianity, as well as other genuine religions that vied for loyalty with the totalitarian states each tried to construct.

The kind of fusion we want to discuss in this section is that in which a particular religion — in this case Christianity — is used for political ends. Oddly enough, sometimes separationists or selective separationists[1] are most adept at sensing the political use of religion, which is one form of what we will be calling fusionism, the undue combining of religion and politics. David Domke and Kevin Coe, in a recent book titled *The God Strategy: How Religion Became a Political Weapon in America* (Oxford University Press, 2008), are alarmed at what they believe to be a dangerous tendency to use religion for political purposes. They firmly believe that certain politicians and political movements have enfolded religion into their political purposes, thereby concocting an unholy and dangerous brew.

> On issue after issue, US public debate today includes — and often is dominated by — faith-based perspectives es-

---

1. I consider Domke and Coe on the surface to be separationists because they heartily endorse John Kennedy's commitment to an "absolute" separation of church and state, which seems to apply also to the interaction of religion and politics (p. 139), and because they confine religion to lofty, "sacred visions" (p. 149), which inspire and comfort but are of a distinctly different color than politics (p. 149). Yet I believe that like so many alleged separationists, they are finally selective separationists. Though they seem to decry liberal use of religion for political purposes, they are alarmed mostly about the effective alliance between conservative religion and conservative politics. Their book has "traced the development of a powerful alliance between religious and political conservatives that worked for decades — with occasional fractures — to transform the nation, its political communications, and its public policies" (p. 150). Indeed, they are alarmed that continuing such a combination will be "fatal to this nation's future" (p. 141).

poused by politically adept individuals and organizations. . . . Political leaders have taken advantage of and con-
tributed to these developments by calculated, deliberate,
and partisan use of faith. We call this the *God Strategy*. (p. 7)

Later we will reflect on whether these authors' claims are justified, but for the moment we will endorse their assessment that
religion can and has become the tool of politics, thereby having
its transcendent nature reduced to the mere instrument of
worldly agents. The political use of religion can take a number of
forms, which we will discuss in turn. The first use is character-
ized by pure cynicism. The leaders of political movements themselves have no real belief in the claims of religion. Indeed, they
may be contemptuous of religion and its claims. But they find
they can make political gains by using or appealing to religion.
The authors cited above seem to think that much political use of
religion in America is cynical. They especially suspect that is the
case with conservatives.

There are many cases that seem to be exercises in cynicism.
No doubt political strategists of both a conservative and liberal
sort calculate just how much religious themes and claims can be
politically useful. They do so without believing in those claims
themselves. For example, when Democrats in the election of
2004 realized that they were losing votes because of their appar-
ent neglect of or hostility toward religion, they changed tactics
and uncomfortably began using religious themes and claims for
themselves. Howard Dean and John Kerry were never very plausi-
ble in their clumsy efforts to make use of religion. Lee Atwater, a
hard-nosed Republican strategist, no doubt co-opted religion for
Republican purposes. Coe and Domke believe that conservatives
— beginning with Nixon and his "Southern Strategy" — have re-
lentlessly and ceaselessly made calculated use of the Christian
faith to gain political power for conservatives. Many liberals be-

lieve that Karl Rove was particularly adept at using religion for conservative political ends.

No doubt a good number of these claims are true, though they may be more ambiguous than the authors suggest. But these transgressions seem mild compared to the cynical use of religion by the authentically evil leaders and movements in history.

Take, for example, Stalin's use of Russian Orthodoxy to strengthen the Soviet Union's wartime resolve against Nazi Germany. Both Lenin and Stalin were implacable persecutors of Christians and Jews, but especially of Russian Orthodox believers. Tens of thousands of priests were executed by Lenin's orders during and in the aftermath of the Bolshevik revolution. The persecution continued unabated under Stalin. The only remnants of the church that were allowed to exist were those who were under the complete control of the totalitarian government. However, when the Soviet Union was under severe threat from the Nazis' armed advance into its territory, Stalin made a calculated decision to relax persecution and use Orthodoxy to rally Russians to greater efforts against the Nazis. As soon as victory over the Nazis was assured, persecution was reinstituted.

Similarly, Hitler persecuted Christians who resisted the rise of the Nazis to power in 1930s Germany. Of course, his persecution of Jews was far worse. He made it clear that the neo-paganism that drove his mad vision was in sharp conflict with Christianity and Judaism. But when he needed more enthusiasm for his war efforts he tried to co-opt Christians by sounding supportive of Christian themes. He tried to use Christianity for his own political and military projects.

This cynical use of religion has been exercised since the beginning of history. Political actors want legitimation and support for their efforts. They are willing to use the language of ultimacy for their own very worldly ends. In fact, many conflicts in history that on the surface appear to be religious conflicts were at root political struggles in which religion was used to further the needs of political actors. Some historians believe that Constantine used Christianity to gain imperial power in the third century AD. Kings and queens, princes and princesses, cardinals and archbishops used religion to further political claims throughout the Middle Ages. The contending parties during the Reformation made much use of religion to further political agendas. The so-called Wars of Religion are better understood as the conflicts between nascent states than genuine conflicts between religions, though there is little doubt that religious authorities allowed themselves to be co-opted by those political powers. Even in the present day, many seemingly religious conflicts — the struggle between Protestants and Catholics in Ireland, the bloodshed between the Catholics of Croatia and the Orthodox of Serbia, for example — feature the cynical use of religion by the political powers that be.

Such depredations can easily lead believers and secularists alike to commit themselves to the total separation of religion and politics. It has even been argued that Christians should keep their identity secret when they enter the political sphere in order to prevent the political use of religion. But, as we argued earlier, separationism is neither possible nor preferable. It truncates religion and impoverishes politics. Indeed, later I shall argue that much of what appears to be the political use of religion is actually the political expression of genuine religious perspective and values, though it is admittedly difficult to distinguish one from the other.

### B. Religious and Ethnic/National Identity Fused

A closely related fusion of religion occurs when religious ideas and ethos so penetrate a culture that the two become symbiotically united. In this case, religion is not simply used as a political tool, though many political actors go ahead and do precisely that. Rather, we are talking of historic communities that have been so influenced by a religious tradition that the two are intertwined, making it difficult to think of one without the other. For example, Icelanders have been Lutherans for centuries. To be an Icelander means to be a Lutheran. The same fusion has happened in many countries and with many ethnic groups and tribes. Croats are Catholics, Serbs are Orthodox, Bosnians are Muslim, Greeks are Orthodox, Scots are Presbyterians, English are Anglicans, and so forth. Some of this fusion is rather harmless and even wholesome, when each serves the other as a source of identity. Religion becomes the font of many of the cultural values of the nation or ethnic group. The nation or ethnic group prizes its religious tradition. In such cases, religion and politics also become deeply interconnected, with ambiguous results.

Will Herberg claimed in his famous book *Protestant, Catholic, Jew* that to be an American meant to be a member of one of those faith groups. National identity and religious commitment coincided. The problem with this sort of fusion is that often the ethnic or national identity gets the best of Christian identity over time. The prophetic elements of the faith are dampened and the faith becomes more and more a comforting blanket to be thrown over national or ethnic identity. Then when conflicts arise among the tribes or nations they resort to those identities rather than their Christian identities. If indeed Christian identity had transcended and been stronger than national and ethnic identity in many of the bloody conflicts of history, there would have been much less blood. But the fusion almost always serves the nation or tribe or ethnic group rather than the faith. Indeed, what the separationists often blame religion for — violence and oppression — is more often the result of the instrumental use of religion by other power centers.

So, while there may be a genuine expression of the faith in the cultural forms of nations and groups, it is dangerous to the faith and to the nations to amalgamate them into one whole. The fusion destroys the needed prophetic and universal elements of the faith while it gives too much sacred legitimation to the needs of the nation, tribe, or ethnic group.

### C. Straight-Line Thinking (Intentional)

There is another sort of fusionism that is very different from the cynical political use of religion, or religion's expression in the communal life of the nation, tribe, or ethnic group. The examples in part A featured persons and movements who generally did not believe in the religion they were using, but rather used it as a tool. In part B religion is organically fused with communities by historic interpenetration. In the examples we will now take up, the persons and movements believe in the religion they are fusing with politics. They believe that there is so much affinity between the central claims of the faith they hold and their favored political policies that the two are scarcely distinguishable. And, contrary to the kinds of fusion in part B, the relation of religion to politics is directed to specific programs and policies, not expressed through the formation of historic communities over time.

In his *Socialist Decision,* Paul Tillich argued that "Socialism is the only possible economic system from the Christian point of view." He drew a straight line from central Christian religious and moral claims to a particular kind of political/economic system, more or less baptizing that system with unequivocal Christian affirmation. He thought the affinities between those central claims and the theoretical and practical thrust of socialism were so close that he was willing to make the argument that Christianity necessarily leads to democratic socialism as a political economic system. And, as a highly intelligent and educated theologian, Tillich was certainly intentional in drawing that straight line. Many Christian intellectuals have followed Tillich's path, claiming that Christianity and socialism are not only compatible, but in fact necessary complements.

Two personal experiences illustrate contemporary straight-line thinking of an intentional sort. For example, this intentional fusion was evident in a Lutheran Ethicists' Conference in which I criticized the tendency of our church's advocacy offices always to endorse liberal policies. In my paper I asked rhetorically: Do Christian ethical norms always lead to liberal policies? One of the veteran Lutheran ethicists responded to my rhetorical question by saying: "Of course, they do; Christian ethics always leads in a 'progressive' direction."

A second example. After offering a sharp public criticism that the new Evangelical Lutheran Church in America was adopting many ideas from the left wing of the Democratic Party such as quotas, equality of results, multiculturalism, feminism, etc., I was confronted by a fellow voting member to its 1989 Church Wide Assembly. "Bob," she said, "you are right in your analysis. Our church is getting many of its identifying themes from the left wing of the Democratic Party. The difference between you and me is that I applaud that connection. You lament it." She was right. I did lament the fusion of the new church with ideas of the left wing of the Democratic Party, but not because it was left-wing. I hope I would have been just as upset with a fusion of the church's main themes with conservative political ideas. Straight-line thinking of both a left- and a right-wing sort are damaging to both religion and politics, especially religion. And to put forth such fusion intentionally is terribly worrisome. It collapses the critical distance that Christian faith must maintain from all worldly sources and expressions of wisdom and power.

Elements of the so-called Religious Right exhibit such straight-line thinking. The very name "Christian Coalition," for example, suggests that a coalition formed to support specific conservative public policies is "Christian." Persons or organizations who do not support those policies are by implication non-Christian. Likewise, the Moral Majority organization of the 80s seemed to imply that those who supported different policies were immoral. The Rev. Jerry Falwell often connected being Christian with support of the Republican agenda. Indeed, the "selective separationists" that I wrote about earlier believe that nearly all Christian conservatives draw such straight lines. There is a veritable cottage industry of books that rant about the influence of religious conservatives on the politics of America, in each case arguing that conservative religion has melded or has been melded into conservative politics. These books are hardly impartial; they rarely worry about liberal religion being conflated into liberal politics. This shows that religious conservatives have indeed made something of an impact on American politics, and these writers do not like it!

Damon Linker *(Theocons: Secular America Under Siege)* believes that a cadre of Catholic conservatives led by (the late) Father Richard John Neuhaus is far along the way in setting up a theocracy in America. Kevin Phillips *(The Peril and Politics of Radical Religion, Oil, and Borrowed Money in the 21st Century)* believes that evangelical and fundamentalist Christians wedded themselves to the Bush agenda and supplied the needed votes to keep it going. Charles Marsh *(Wayward Christian Soldiers: Freeing the Gospel from Political Captivity)* believes that American evangelicals have sold their birthright to Republican politics by supporting the Iraq War. In *American Fascists: The Christian Right and the War on America,* Christopher Hedges takes the tiny Restorationist or Dominion movement among conservative Christians as somehow a bellwether of things to come. Michelle Goldberg in

*Kingdom Coming: The Rise of Christian Nationalism* takes a similar line. Mark L. Taylor finds that religious conservatives have succumbed to the worst temptations of power and empire in his *Religion, Politics, and the Christian Right: Post 9/11 Powers in the American Empire.* Mainline Protestant groups suspect that the Institute on Religion and Democracy draws such straight lines and thus runs interference for conservative politics. There are no doubt people in these conservative circles who believe that to be a Christian necessarily means to support the conservative political agenda, and their mere existence has brought forth these overwrought charges. But as a general case against conservatives, these diatribes are unconvincing.

It is not as if there were no connection between those central claims of the faith and political philosophies and politics. There certainly are, or we would have to admit that the separationists are right. But the problem is that the connections between the central claims and political policies are too certain and confident — too straight a line is drawn. Rather, one must traverse a number of links in an argument to move from those central claims to specific public policies. Each link provides an opportunity for Christians of good will and intelligence to disagree on the movement from the center to public policy. Factors other than faith-claims enter into that movement. One's political philosophy, ordering of values, political culture, social class, level of education, and reading of the empirical situation enter into a complete argument along with the religious values. Later we shall sketch out what such a movement might look like, but at the moment we merely need to say that the connection should not be too tight or confident.

34

## D. Straight-Line Thinking (Unintentional)

The vast majority of Christians would react with horror to the claim that faith in and obedience to God means following the policies of the Republican Party, or, for that matter, the Democratic Party. Most Christians have respect enough for the transcendent and universal claims of the gospel that they would blanch at making such tight connections. They believe the church's mission is to preach the gospel of forgiveness directed to all repentant souls, not to promote a political program equated with the gospel. So every church refuses to make such overt equations.

Yet, many individuals and churches are so deeply committed to the affinity of their faith convictions with particular political philosophies and programs that they de facto fuse the faith and politics. What they would deny in theory they perform in practice. We have already mentioned the many charges against evangelicals that they have wedded their faith to conservative politics. The critics often imply that this is intentional, but few of the accused would admit to such intentional fusion. If there is fusion, and there is evidence that evangelicals are not as monolithic politically as the critics claim, it is mostly of the unintentional sort.

Likewise with the mainstream Protestants. Though no mainstream Protestant church would theologically equate core Christian affirmations with liberal politics, they actually equate them in practice. Take, for example, the advocacy office (Lutheran Office of Governmental Affairs) of my own church, the Evangelical Lutheran Church in America. The church takes a specific position on scores of issues. The church accepts the alleged global warming consensus and supports all sorts of government interventions to diminish carbon dioxide in the air. It is in favor of a Climate Security Bill proposed by Senators Lieberman and

Warner. It is against the separation wall in Israel and for a shared Jerusalem. It is against the new NAFTA arrangements with Latin America. It pressed for the Affordable Housing Trust Fund which purports to make housing more available to those less able to pay. (This was before the housing crisis brought on by too many high-risk housing loans.) It supports across-the-board debt cancellation to poor countries. It is for the Farm Bill. It is for renewable energy to make electricity, but not for nuclear power. It has inveighed against the war in Iraq and wants to end military operations in Iraq as soon as "responsibly possible." It is for increasing foreign aid by the government. Its bishop has lectured the prospective presidents of the USA on how to improve America and the world, most of his suggestions involving government interventions to redistribute wealth. Little is said about the challenge of creating wealth, especially in a country that is experiencing an economic contraction.

On each of these issues the church's positions are the same positions as those one would expect from the Democratic Party. And, interestingly, the public issues that many conservative Lutherans are interested in — restraint of abortion, stem cell research, protection-of-marriage amendments, legal protection for private schools and home schooling, some restraint over media portrayals of sex and violence — none of these appear on the ELCA agenda.

Other mainstream Protestant churches — Episcopal, Presbyterian, Methodist — exhibit similar characteristics. Their preferred policies seem to mimic those of the Democratic Party. Yet, their membership is not nearly as monolithically liberal as the preferred policies would suggest. Indeed, conservatives within those churches are often aggravated by the official church claiming to speak for them. Yet, the advocacy offices plunge forward.

What is going on? It seems that though the churches know that the central claims of the faith cannot be directly translated into liberal political positions, they go ahead and do just that. What seems to be happening is that this translation goes on unintentionally. Non-theological factors intervene to make the movement from central claims to liberal political policies obvious and seamless, when in fact such a movement is neither obvious nor seamless. The line is not as straight as the advocates believe.

As we pointed out earlier, the Religious Right often offers a reverse mirror image of this obvious and seamless movement, only this time from central core convictions to conservative policies. Perhaps most of their straight-line thinking is unintentional, too, just as that of the Protestant mainline. In each case it is difficult to sort out where conscious intention ends and unconscious assumption begins.

The same things can be said about the tendencies of individuals unconsciously or unintentionally to fuse their Christian convictions with their political preferences. While most individual Christians know theoretically that the gospel transcends political division, they have a hard time making that distinction in practice. Such fusion has the potential for separating Christians from each other in a lamentable way. Perhaps that is why most local parishes stay away from political discussion in their programs. They fear that people who have fused their religion and politics will not be able to engage in civil discourse with other Christians who have fused them in a different way. Too much ultimate legitimation is given to their political opinions to allow persons to converse civilly.

At any rate, much fusion between religion and politics goes on among religious bodies and individuals in the United States. Such fusion is damaging to the transcendent claims of faith, making them instead suspiciously consonant with partisan political perspectives of a very earthly and secular sort. While such fusion damages politics less than it does religion, it does add an aura of absoluteness to policies that are anything but certain.

Let us now turn constructively to a better way of thinking about religion and politics in which the two are neither separated nor fused.

*Chapter Four*

# Critical Engagement:
# Moving from Core to Public Policy

Now that we have shown the two basic bad ways of relating religion and politics — separationism and fusion, it is now time to move to the constructive task. How do the central claims of Christianity relate to the mundane realities of political life? If there is no straight line from one to the other, what then is the relationship of those Christian claims to specific political policies? To answer this question, we will first have to outline what the central claims of the faith are. What are at its core? What is it that engages political policy? Then we will examine how one moves from that core to public policy.

## A. Theological Essentials

For Christians the flaming center at the core of the faith is the event of Jesus Christ — his birth, teachings, ministry, death, and resurrection. Jesus Christ not only teaches and preaches truths about God and his will; he enacts those truths in a ministry of judgment, healing, forgiveness, and instruction about how to live obediently before God. In so doing he reveals God's will toward us as fallen human beings who are yet capable of rescue.

But Jesus goes beyond conveying revelatory knowledge about God; he claims and does things that only God can claim and do. This gets him into deep trouble with religious and political authorities, and they conspire to get rid of him. He is gruesomely executed on a cross. But that ignominious cross is at the same time the instrument of Christ's saving work that reconciles humans to God by taking into himself (and therefore into God himself) the consequences of sin and in so doing exhausts the power of sin to estrange us from God. His bodily resurrection vindicates his claims and demonstrates his (and God's) triumph over sin, death, and the devil. After his resurrection he appears to his depressed followers and sparks a new beginning of faith in him and his work.

It is important not to sentimentalize this core. Jesus' teachings are not simply about love. He first sharpens and radicalizes the law of God by applying it to the internal motivations of humans. A man who lusts consistently after another woman is guilty of adultery, just as is the one who acts out that lust. This sharpening of the law brings low all human beings. "Before God no one can stand." But to the repentant sinner, Jesus offers God's forgiving love. The Prodigal Son, once he is clear about his sinfulness, is greeted by his loving father and restored to the family. But then forgiven sinners are expected to pass on the love that gave them a second chance, even as the foreign Good Samaritan showed compassion to the Jew who had been felled by robbers. God's radical love in Christ — inclusive, unconditional, steadfast, forgiving, biased toward the vulnerable — restores and renews mortal sinners so they might pass that love on to others. Such love — agape love — is the crown of Christian ethics.

That love is what gives the Commandments of God an indeterminately positive thrust. The Commandments prohibit certain actions contrary to love, but the divine love behind them opens them up to a creative thrust that goes the second mile.

Those who live the Christian life are called to reflect that love in their worldly callings in some way. Likewise, the church conveys that love and holds it up as a transcendent ethical norm that judges all earthly efforts to fulfill it even while it spurs higher achievements of love and justice.

One of the crucial implications of this norm is that each person matters; each is viewed as precious in God's sight, no matter how flawed or degraded he or she might be. This has enormous, but indirect, implications for politics. Later we shall outline some of those implications.

However, Christianity is not first of all a religion of moral obligation or achievement. It is essentially a religion of salvation, one in which God reaches out in Christ with saving grace for repentant souls. It is about God's gratuitous, loving action in Christ, not about our work. Thus, it is profoundly true that Christianity is first of all not a political religion; it is about God's action in Christ, not ours. It is only when one includes the human response — both individual and communal — to that action that we get the moral force that has implications for politics. The radical grace of God in Christ comes from the outside — from God's dimension into ours — and transcends all worldly borders and fault-lines. It is offered to all repentant sinners, regardless of their politics. Those who are "in him" are gathered by Christ into that mystical Body of Christ that will persist beyond this world into the eternal life of the Trinity.

But if Christianity offered to politics only the transcendent norm of agape love for each human being, it would come to politics with only a narrow, though very important, message. Christianity comes with much more, because the Christ event of the New Testament cannot be understood without the revelation and action of God chronicled in the Old Testament. It also comes with the wisdom given the Christian community in the coming of the Holy Spirit told about in the Book of Acts, which gift

41

persists in shaping Christian wisdom throughout the ages. Christianity comes to politics with the freight of the whole Trinitarian faith.

What are some of the key insights of the Old Testament? Certainly the fact that God has created the world and pronounced it good is essential. The world is not an eternal reality separate from God, nor is it to be identified with him. It — with its many creatures — is God's good creation. It is a gift to be tended and stewarded, not exploited thoughtlessly. As the crown of creation God created male and female, who together are made in his image. That image means that they have the capacity for loving relationships with God and each other, as well as the gifts of freedom, self-transcendence, and reason. Even before the Fall, God gives the two the First Institution — marriage. In that primal covenant they are called to "cling to each other" in love and fidelity and replenish the earth through children. Together they have dominion over the earth and its creatures as stewards of God. They are also something very special before God — they have sacred worth.

Sadly, humans were tempted and fell. They rebelled from the Creator and tried to exalt themselves to godlike proportions. They radically disrupted their relationships to God, to each other, to themselves, and to the creation. Though created in the image of God and therefore good, they are fallen. Their fundamental predicament is not one of ignorance, but one of sin — willful separation from God, each other, and the creation. Since that primeval rebellion humans have been infected with original sin, which means that their wills are incurved upon themselves. They are unable to recover the disrupted relations to God and each other by themselves. They are in bondage to an inescapable pride that becomes even more disruptive when it works its way through large groups or organizations.

The Old Testament recounts the efforts of God to retrieve his lost creation. The call of Abraham begins the great story, in which God promises that through Abraham and his children the world will be blessed. After many twists and turns, the children of Israel find themselves bound as slaves in Egypt. But God raises up Moses who leads them out of bondage. Immediately after freeing them from the Egyptian pharaohs, God forges a covenant with Israel in which he will be their God and they will be his people. He not only frees them out of his gracious love for them, but he gives them a set of guidelines — the Ten Commandments — that will enable them to live in harmony and shalom with God and each other. This is the Law, which indeed is part of the blessing that God gives to the world through Israel. The Law becomes a moral compass for all of human history, including political life. This Law, revealed clearly in the Commandments, is built into the creation; its natural patterns can be discerned by human reason.

The ensuing story of Israel is one of falling away, repentance, exile, and homecoming. Through it all God is calling his people to return to him. But it finally doesn't work. The prophets hold up their mirror to Israel, showing them how they repeatedly fail to keep their covenant with God and each other and therefore are constantly brought to judgment. However, besides words of judgment, the prophets also bring words of hope. They predict another great rescue mission in history, one that will reclaim the lost creation. Acting out of steadfast love, God will send a Messiah who will bring healing to a creation that cannot heal itself. The prophets create a great sense of expectation among the people of Israel. It is into that expectant context that Jesus of Nazareth appears.

So the event of Christ has a prehistory that makes it intelligible. Through Christ, God reaches out again for his lost creation. Sin is overcome, not by human righteousness, but through the mercy of God in Christ. The Law that sinful humans could not

43

fulfill was fulfilled by Christ. God liberates his creation. God the Father and God the Son are active in these histories. However, the story does not end there. After the resurrection when the disciples are meeting to share stories of Jesus and his appearances to them, a mighty Spirit invades them and brings them together into one body, the church, which then is sent out to bring the news of God's liberation in Christ to the world. A new movement begins with only a few passionate followers, but soon blossoms into a massive movement that penetrates the known world with its religious and moral message. The Spirit works through history, gathering a people to God through Christ, and then sending them out to proclaim the good news to all. From the beginning onward, the ongoing activity of God as Father, Son, and Holy Spirit works to sustain and finally liberate the whole creation. This is the magnificent drama of redemption that is wrought by the sovereign triune God. At the end of time Christ will come again as judge and savior, and God will bring forth a new creation to be enjoyed by those whom he claims as his own. Until then, God sustains and governs his creation through his law while the church does its work.

Bearing this message, the church then expands to many nations and peoples. It becomes an institution and founds many more. It shapes the political, economic, social, and cultural life of the West, as well as many other parts of the world in which it gains ground. It draws upon the key convictions that lie at its theological core, which we have tried to outline. The church builds up an intellectual and moral tradition based upon that core, and imparts that tradition to its laity throughout the ages.

The upshot of this in the West is that Christianity has pervasively conditioned political life. Sometimes, when it had political power, it did so directly. But mostly the effects were indirect, wherein Christian individuals and groups carried those core intellectual and moral convictions with them into political life, both as political leaders and ordinary citizens.[1] The church now finds itself in a post-Christendom era in which it no longer expects or is allowed to exercise coercive political power. But its core convictions still drive both individual Christians and the church into engagement with the political world.

## B. Politically Relevant Principles from the Core

The preceding depiction of the core of Christian belief is basically narrative in form, far from giving specific direction to political life. So, the first step among several in moving from core to periphery is to distill principles from that core that are relevant to politics. This is, of course, a step out from that core that involves a good deal of interpretation. Christians of good will and intelligence, as well as Christians from differing traditions, would perhaps derive different principles — though perhaps not radically different — from the core. In addition, many would order them differently, placing them in different hierarchies than I have done. (I have already argued in Chapter One that the very

---

1. One of the major indirect influences of Christianity on political life in America has been its likening of the American story with the biblical drama of redemption. From the beginning of American history, Christians have seen God building the kingdom of God in America, just as he did in the story of Israel. America was seen to be a chosen people, which God elected, called, judged, and renewed. H. Richard Niebuhr traces this American tendency in his *The Kingdom of God in America.* This has given America enormous capacities for reform and renewal, while at the same time given it the occasion for disappointment and despair. But from our Lutheran point of view, the whole scheme of likening America to Israel is a dubious one. America is not God's instrument of salvation; only the gospel borne by the church is. It will never be built by us into the kingdom of God, which is a prideful and parochial notion. Rather, America — as are all nations — is a provisional structure sustained by God for maintaining security, order, and justice. America is important as an earthly kingdom, not as the kingdom of God.

nature of the faith itself drives Christians toward engagement with politics; complete separation is simply not an option.)


## 1. Humans as Exalted but Fallen

Glen Tinder, in his book *The Political Meaning of Christianity* (Louisiana State University, 1989), summarizes his argument: "It is hardly too much to say that the idea of the exalted individual is the spiritual center of Western politics" (p. 33). This idea, he believes, pushes governments to be respectful of each individual, egalitarian, and universalist. Earlier in his book, Tinder grounds the "exalted individual" in both its creation in the image of God and its redemption by the work of Christ.

I believe Tinder has it exactly right. The value of each individual, established in his creation and redemption, is the central value of Western democratic ideology and practice at its best. Though refracted through Enlightenment categories, this biblical affirmation of the value of each individual lies behind our notion of the rights and freedoms of the individual, government by consent, equality before the law, and a host of policies that protect, offer justice, and aid persons when they are in distress. This affirmation of the "exalted individual" comes from beyond the state; it is anchored in ultimate reality — God. Therefore, governments do not invent or generate the value of the individual; they recognize what is prior to them logically and ontologically. When governments do not recognize this value, Christians have both the grounds and the obligation to resist them and their policies. Just as there is a transcendent ground for anchoring human value and rights, so too there is a transcendent ground for Christian moral obligation. "We must obey God rather than men" when it comes to direct conflict between God's will and earthly policies that contradict that will.

Thus, governments that recognize this transcendent value must treat individuals with respect. Persons are ends in themselves, never solely means for something or someone. This fundamental value has great implications for politics, though rarely can a straight line be drawn from this value to specific public policy. But for many Christians it does generate strong resistance to abortion, the use of embryos in scientific research, and torture. It also generates commitments to make medical care and basic shelter and food accessible to the most vulnerable among us. Again, however, many other considerations complicate matters.

One complicating matter is that the idea of the freedom and dignity of the individual means that government observes the rights of people to make their own free choices about important matters as long as they do not do serious harm to others. Respecting freedom means allowing a good deal of "freedom from" governmental interference, even when the choices the individual makes are sometimes not good. Too much paternalism not only does not respect that freedom; it sometimes undermines freedom and dignity by making the individual dependent upon the state — hence the long-standing argument about how much individuals should be responsible for themselves in important matters, and how much the state should take responsibility for them, and perhaps from them. Precisely within the Christian understanding of human nature is a disagreement about how human freedom and dignity should be respected. Modern political liberals tend to emphasize the paternalist role in the economic sphere while political conservatives tend to prefer policies that maximize freedom. With regard to social and cultural life, the tendencies are reversed: liberals press for freedom while conservatives favor regulation.

An even more important complicating factor is that the Christian view of human nature not only affirms man as good, but also as finite and fallen. Finitude means that humans have physical, emotional, and spiritual limits set by God that are transgressed only at great peril. Thus, too much manipulation of human physicality is fraught with danger, though part of our finitude is not knowing exactly what is "too much." How much should we try to expand the finite span of our lives, for example? Certainly Christians are not likely to believe in earthly immortality. How much shall we genetically shape "perfect" human specimens? Most Christians shrink from such a prospect. On the other hand, those same Christians believe in using medicine and surgical interventions to save and extend life . . . within limits. Finitude also means that humans cannot do and be all things to all people. They have very important, but limited, responsibilities to their own spouses, families, neighborhoods, cities, and countries. Forfeiting their particular responsibilities to universal ones is hazardous.

Finitude means that humans have a legitimate self-interest in taking care of themselves and those near to them. When that self-interest is respected and engaged, humans tend better to fulfill their responsibilities to themselves and others. This is one of the sources of the famous Catholic doctrine of subsidiarity — getting important tasks done should be located at the lowest feasible social strata. If the individual or single family can get the task done, the city or the state should not usurp that function.

Legitimate self-interest also means that persons can take care of themselves and their nearest social relations well enough so that they might have enough energy and wealth left over to serve others.

Self-interest of this sort also drives economies, both on the producer and consumer side of the ledger. Legitimate self-interest can properly lead to profit-seeking on the producer side and reasonable consumption on the other.

Human finitude is complicated further by human sinfulness.

Humans are good, but fallen. They are inevitably corrupted by a will incurved upon themselves, making themselves out to be little gods. Sin turns legitimate self-interest into selfishness. This corruption leads humans to faulty and fractured relations with God, others, themselves, and the creation. When the world's underlying moral order is violated, there are distinct repercussions. Sin brings wrath.

The basic human problem therefore is neither ignorance nor general finitude; it is sin — willfully separating themselves from those to whom they should be in covenantal relations. What's more, they cannot overcome this bondage by themselves. The Holy Spirit must break this bondage and open them to the reconciling gospel of Christ, which alone can heal the ruptured relations. Even when Christians receive the gospel and through the Spirit lead a Christian life, the old sin in them does not die completely. They will struggle with sin until their deaths. Perfection in this life is not theirs to enjoy.

This fallenness is even more magnified in the life of groups and organizations. Lacking the capacity for repentance and salvation possible for individuals, as well as gathering far more power than individuals, groups and organizations are apt to be far more inordinately self-interested than individuals. When the social aggregate is large enough, as in the nation state, it is inevitable that self-interest will be expressed in heavy and sometimes damaging ways. Large social aggregates will inevitably exhibit human sin in exaggerated fashion. Thus, unchecked power is always a liability from a Christian point of view.

This Christian doctrine of sin has enormous political implications. For one thing, humans cannot look to the state or government for salvation or liberation, as a number of totalitarian regimes have promised. Not only is the state itself infected with human sin and therefore incapable of redeeming lost human beings; it tends to claim way too much for itself. It has a great propensity toward idolatry. Therefore, citizens must be protected from the overweening power of the state by other powerful checks, such as constitutional law. The government must be limited by the consent of the governed. In international relations, great powers must be checked by other limiting powers. Reinhold Niebuhr was particularly wise in showing how achieving balances of power among large centers of power is one of the main instruments of earthly justice. Such balances limit the limitless self-will of large entities.

On the individual level, human sin can often lead to individual irresponsibility. Without accountability, humans often willfully take advantage of others and of the state's efforts to support them. Pride and sloth are both the products of sinful human nature. Thus, good public policy not only must respect the "exalted individual" by treating him or her with respect and justice; it must also allow for his or her freedom, and arrange disincentives to keep him or her from becoming dependent on others and the state.

All these complications involved in trying to outline the political relevance of the Christian doctrine of human nature might lead one to despair of any clear relevance whatever. Certainly it does lead to a decent respect for the difficult craft of drafting good public policy. Taking all these complications into account is a daunting challenge. Yet, there are some fairly clear directions suggested by our summary of the Christian view of human nature and its predicament.

This Christian view sets sharp limits on political claims. It prohibits intentional mistreatment of persons. It is very skeptical of taking innocent life. It augurs for fairness for all, especially the least fortunate. It demands a sphere of freedom for the profound decisions of life — religious, familial, marital, vocational. It makes room for conscientious objection. It encourages self-criticism. It resists efforts to "play God" by intentionally ending, reshaping, or redefining human life. It is realistic in its assessment of the nature and actions of large political, economic, and social entities; it proposes limits upon them.

## 2. The Qualitative Distinction Between God's Salvation and All Human Efforts

If the preceding theological exposition was at all compelling, it should be clear that Christians look for liberation or salvation from their predicament — their bondage to sin — by the work of God in Jesus Christ that is proclaimed in and through the church. God reigns among them by his Word, to which they freely consent. Salvation is a free gift of God in Christ. Before God with regard to their salvation, humans are purely receptive. This means that we do not look to political — or economic or social or educational — schemes for salvation.

This seems like a banal assertion, but it is far from that. Humans in groups — particularly in politics — often claim redemptive capacities. Some religious traditions in America have strong notions of sanctification for the individual Christian; they ascribe near perfection to their new lives in the Spirit. They then transfer that notion of personal sanctification to social and political movements that they instigate and participate in. They claim to be building God's kingdom on earth. While the religious roots of such transformative-minded groups have often been excised in the modern world, even secular reform groups claim that they are redeeming the world through human effort. All sorts of groups make such claims, from self-help groups to revolutionary movements to powerful nations. When the God-man (Jesus Christ) is rejected, the man-god rushes in to take his place.

We have many massive examples of such claims. The Enlightenment claimed to bring the heavenly city to earth through reason and science; Marxist-Leninist movements offered promises to bring paradise to earth through revolution; Nazis attempted to establish a thousand-year Reich. The latter two, sometimes termed "bastard children of the Enlightenment" for their claim to be scientifically based, made the twentieth century the bloodiest of all centuries through their arrogant political messianism.

While there are few current examples of explicit political messianism, there are many muted and subdued claims. Militant environmentalism promises a sustainable world of harmony with nature, albeit with a lot fewer humans. "Saving the earth" has a good claim on becoming a new candidate for inflated — and possibly oppressive — political claims. Remnants of liberation theology make the gospel into "revolutionary practice." Our own political parties and candidates use a rhetoric that borders on messianic at times. Above all, education makes veiled claims about its liberating capacities that are often believed by its political patrons. Pathetically, celebrity culture promises salvation through fifteen minutes of fame or at least participation in the aura of celebrities, some of them collective in nature.

Authentic Christian faith brings politics down to earth where it belongs. That does not make it unimportant, for God has chosen to reign in another way in addition to his reign by the gospel in the hearts of individuals and the church. Though God's gift of salvation is the pearl of great price offered from above — vertically, as it were — to believing Christians, he also reigns horizontally through his Law, in all those earthly agencies that preserve order and justice on earth, politics being a key one of those agencies. God's reign in the horizontal dimension does not bring salvation, but it does aim for as much order and justice as possible in a finite and fallen world. What's more, non-Christians are often as constructive and fruitful as Christians in pursuit of worldly order and justice. They often possess as much or more practical wisdom and political courage as Christians. Further, while God's reign through the gospel is one of persuasion and love, his reign through the Law uses coercive power when need be. A fallen world cannot be governed simply by persuasion, though it needs as much of that as possible.

Politics — the work of the state or government — is then fully honored from this point of view. As St. Paul says in Romans 13, government has been instituted by God to support good conduct while punishing the bad. The governor is the "servant for your good" (13:4). Christians not only must pay taxes; they can also participate vigorously in government. They can rightly expect and press government to give protection to its citizens from internal and external threats, to work for international order and justice commensurate with the power that it possesses, to encourage and monitor wisely a vibrant economy, to forge reasonable policies to conserve our habitat, to pursue justice for all (which includes safeguarding freedoms as well as providing an adequate safety net for those unable to care for themselves), and to exhibit and support humane values.

Government is seen as an instrument of God for preserving a basic order and justice that enables people to live and flourish. It ensures time and space for the church to proclaim the gospel, the church's central mission. All of these proper ends of government, however, are stated as abstract generalizations. There are yet a number of important moves to be made in order to concretize them into policy. And with each move Christians of good will and intelligence — along with other citizens with the same qualities — can disagree. Yet, we have distilled several important Christian principles from core convictions: government, while ordained by God, cannot be an instrument of salvation. God uses other means for that — the church and its gospel of Christ. Government itself deeply participates in and magnifies the fallenness of human nature. Because it is powerful, it must be held in check and constantly scrutinized.

What can be expected then from government is not heaven on earth, but a gradual progression of small steps toward a better society. The realism of the Christian faith rejoices in those small steps even as it doubts political promises of wholesale transformation toward utopia. There can indeed be progress, but there can also be regress. There is no automatic movement upwards. What's more, it is in the real world of politics that accurate, relative distinctions become highly important. Because no society can achieve anything close to utopia, it is important not to judge societies by utopian standards and thereby fall into despair or useless revolutionary illusions. The relatively good and the relatively bad are important distinctions when it comes to political achievement.

God will bring his kingdom when and how he wishes. Humans cannot hasten or even know that moment. When they do claim to bring in the kingdom, they are most likely to bring hell. Christians do expect that the end will be full of conflict and finally end in a judgment in which God will unerringly sort things out. At that time what will be important will be how one has responded to the gospel, not one's political allegiances or achievements.

*3. Christian Service*

All classical Christian traditions agree that upon reception of the grace of God in Christ, Christians are to respond in gratitude to God and with loving service to the neighbor in the concrete places of responsibility that God has given them. Christians are called to serve the neighbor as spouses, parents, and children in the private realm, as workers in the economic realm, as citizens in the political realm, as careful stewards of the creation, as volunteers in the social realm, and as faithful members of the church. Indeed, these places of responsibility become precisely the locations where the two ways that God reigns in the world intersect. Those who receive the gospel are under God's reign as they respond in faith, love, and hope toward him, but they also activate that faith, love, and hope toward others in and through the mundane responsibilities of life. Those mundane responsibilities are sustained and governed by God's law operating incognito through the many agencies that organize and guide human life. Christians receiving the love of God through Christ (vertically, as it were) then convey that love through loving service to the neighbor in the world (horizontally, as it were). In this way God sustains and partially restores and heals the world. God uses Christians as salt and leaven in this beautiful but fallen world.

Before we examine lay callings in the world, it is important to indicate that the church has a specific calling or mission in the world. It is entrusted with the Word of God, and its primary responsibility is to proclaim that Word — as both Law and Gospel — to the world. The Holy Spirit will ensure that this living Word will not come back empty. A community will be gathered that will receive both Word and sacrament and be restored, healed, and directed by it. In response to Word and sacrament, the church will worship, build up its members by education and formation, provide a community in which joys and burdens are shared, engage in evangelism and charity, spin off many voluntary organizations to get service done that it cannot do, and also play a public role as a proponent of a wider justice.

The state cannot directly support the church, but it can acknowledge the important work that the church does by giving it free space to do its work. It must be allowed "the free exercise of religion." The state also encourages the supportive work of the church by not taxing it when it performs its proper mission. The state in its three branches should also not confuse separation of church and state, which deals with institutional relationships, with the separation of religion and politics, which deals with the interaction of religious values and perspectives and the political process. The latter is protected by the First Amendment, whose first freedom enables religious persons and institutions to bring their religious values to bear in the political process. Further, such interaction is inevitable when Christians take seriously the comprehensive scope of God's sovereignty and their duty to that sovereign God.

Laypersons are called to serve their neighbors in family life, work, public life (which includes voluntary associations in addition to formal political life), and the church. Each of those "locations" demands non-moral competencies and virtues in order to perform them well. Work as a teacher, for example, means that the teacher knows the material being taught, can communicate it well, and can find encouraging ways to help students learn. The politician must have an inordinate amount of energy, must know how to campaign well, make persuasive arguments, and, above all, propose policy that will be persuasive to his or her colleagues. Christians in government are not excused from mastering those practices and virtues because they are pious believers. Luther famously declared that a good cobbler makes good shoes, not inferior ones with little crosses on them. These requirements indicate that the Christian must pass muster with the worldly demands required in the earthly realm (God's "horizontal reign" through the Law).

There are also moral values that inhere to each location of responsibility, and Christians are expected to possess them also. Indeed, Christian formation in churches often involves training in honesty, integrity, promise-keeping, humility, and reliability, among others. Churches have been the "small platoons" wherein virtue is taught and practiced.

It should be noted that the central Christian traditions maintain that persons other than Christians can master the non-moral and moral values of these places of responsibility. These worldly virtues can be learned and expressed independent of religious involvement and formation. Indeed, these virtues are discussed and promoted in classical pagan literature. Conversely, specifically Christian faith and values do not necessarily prepare the Christian for political office. Non-Christians can often exercise these virtues better than Christians. This does not mean, however, that assessment of political office holders on a number of religious grounds is completely out of bounds. We shall discuss this in due time.

When involved in worldly callings, however, the lay Christian does not simply follow the dictates of the world in these places of responsibility, though she certainly must take account of them. Besides the common moral virtues mentioned above, the Christian also brings the virtues of faith, love, and hope into these places of responsibility. Faith first of all means trust in the saving grace of God in Christ, which frees the Christian from striving for salvation in any effort of his own, including political efforts.

But faith also has practical (horizontal) meanings. First, the Christian has faith that when one performs one's calling competently one is participating in God's sustaining care for the world. For example, work in the economy of a constructive sort is God-pleasing. When one treats the natural world with restraint and respect, one works with the grain of the universe. In these activities, there is a deeper meaning to what one is doing: one is cooperating with God's nurture of his world. Second, one has a sense that one is "assigned" or "called" to this particular worldly activity, whether it be work in the economy, being a good father, participating in the church, or taking on political office. God has roles or purposes in mind for each of us in these worldly activities, and the faithful Christian has a sense of being blessed by God with important purposes in life. He or she has been given roles that give meaning and direction to life. Finally, practical faith means that the Christian trusts that God has revealed important insights about the central issues of life in the history of redemption. Indeed, the first two politically relevant principles we have just discussed in this section — humans as exalted but fallen, the qualitative distinction between God's saving work and our own — are examples of the kinds of insights the Christian brings to political life. Other places of responsibility draw upon other Christian sources of insight. Education, for example, would enter into dialogue with Christian notions of nature and history, human nature and its predicament, and moral traditions such as the just war theory. In other words, Christians bring intellectual and moral insights from the Christian tradition to bear on every activity in their callings, so that they participate critically in them. This is true of Christian participation in family life, work, politics, voluntary associations, and the church.[2] It is also the case both for Christian citizens who make decisions about voting and for Christian politicians who inhabit political office. However, as we have noted above, that "bringing

2. This insistence that Christians bring critical moral and intellectual insights to bear in their worldly callings is something of a revision of most classical Lutheran thinking, in which activity in the left-hand kingdom (what I have been calling the "horizontal" dimension of God's reign) is subject only to reason and experience, both of which are purported to be available to secular people as well as Christians. Without denying the importance of reason and experience, or the capacity of secular persons to work effectively in the horizontal realm, I firmly believe that there are additional insights drawn from the Trinitarian faith as a whole that the Christian brings to bear on each worldly place of responsibility. Shutting out such Christian wisdom denies the Christian tradition specific and relevant intellectual and moral content. Such rejection of Christian wisdom seems to be a formula for the complete secularization of those places of responsibility, as well as the loss of extremely important moral and intellectual criticism and guidance in these important places. But even more importantly, it denies the comprehensive nature of the Christian faith. Or, to put it theologically, it de facto denies the sovereignty of God over all of existence, or at least doubts that we can have any clues about that sovereignty. We are then freed from trying to discern God's will in these places as well as any responsibility for following it.

to bear" is not a simple, straight-line process, but nevertheless one that brings Christian wisdom and morality into play.

Christians as citizens or politicians also bring the virtue of love to bear on their calling. In politics Christian love presses for a greater degree of justice in the world. Serving fellow human beings means a search for those ways to maintain a decent order, alleviate suffering, make opportunities available for others to flourish, and provide for those who cannot help themselves. In America many of these functions are done by voluntary associations, but there is yet great room and responsibility for government to become involved.

Christians also bring hope to their callings, a hope that is not anchored in some thin optimism, but rather hope in the continuing grace, sovereignty, and power of God. They believe that God's continuing grace in their own lives can overcome the paralyzing factors that bedevil us all — the sense of failure and guilt, of insignificance, and of futility. They can begin anew every morning knowing that their sins are forgiven. They need not worry about how important their deeds are because they have hope that God will use them as he wishes. They are confident that they contribute to God's work in the world whether that is visible to them or not. They can be content with small victories because the future is not all up to them. They have hope that God will finally right the things that are wrong in this life, and bring the whole of history to completion. Finally, they live in hope that this life is not all there is. As Christ rose from the dead, so those who are "in Christ" will rise with him on the last day, and joyfully participate in the eternal life of the Trinity.

So, Christians bring faith, hope, and love to their callings as citizens and politicians. They bring not only specific motivations and virtues, but Christian insights derived from the core of Christian belief — the exalted and fallen individual, the difference between God's saving work and our efforts, and Christian service in the world (with its many sub-points). These provide the next step outward from that central core toward public policy. Let us proceed to the next concentric circle in our movement toward specific public policy.

## C. Conditioning Factors in Moving from Core to Public Policy

I argued above that finitude is a characteristic of the human condition, though not its most problematic part. From a Christian point of view, sin is the most damaging part of our predicament as humans. But finitude means that we are inescapably caught in a particular time and place. As H. Richard Niebuhr once put it: "We are not only in time and space; they are in us." There may be elements of human nature that are transcultural and transhistorical, but they are few and far between. Even those universal elements — reason, self-consciousness — are deeply conditioned by culture and history. Grand religious traditions that extend over thousands of years do indeed have much continuity in them, but they also change and develop over time and space. So it is not surprising that the conditioning factors of our own specific time and place will influence us as we try to apply the more continuous elements of our religious tradition to the specific challenges of public policy.

At the same time, however, I would contend that those religious elements cannot be reduced to the cultural and historical factors that condition them. If that were the case, we would have the complete absorption — or, as I earlier called it, "fusion" — of religion into culture or politics. Only in this case the fusion would be completely determined by social factors; religion would serve only as the sacred legitimation of social and political claims, not as a causative factor in itself. As we indicated above,

this absorption or fusion of religion into politics sometimes occurs. But it is certainly not a necessary occurrence. The religious
factor has conditioned politics as well as vice versa.

The realization that our religious convictions are filtered
through a number of conditioning factors should lend a sense of
humility in our movement from core to periphery, however.
What we might on first glance think are religiously grounded political convictions may be at least partly unintentional expressions of other conditioning factors. Indeed, those conditioning
factors affect even our interpretation of the Christian core, if not
the core itself. Yet, I believe that there is an Apostolic Faith that
resides in the core that conveys the revelation of God as Father,
Son, and Holy Spirit. Again, to use an apt image of H. Richard
Niebuhr, even though we see the truth through distorted prisms,
we do not doubt the reality of what we see. God has entered human history from his dimension and revealed himself in the
grand story of redemption.

The following is a partial list of the social factors that condition our move from the Christian core to public policy:

*1. Family Culture and History*

We are brought up in families that often have strong political
viewpoints, even if they are not well articulated. A good deal of
that family culture is inherited from the historical experience of
earlier generations as well as one's own. Catholic ethnic families
have long-held commitments to the Democratic Party, as do
Jews. They began their journey in America as vulnerable minori-
ties and fastened on to political parties that they felt protected
them and enhanced their prospects. My family was heavily affected by the experience of the Great Depression. That experience pressed upon them the virtues of uncomplaining endur-

ance, frugality, sobriety, and vigorous self-reliance. They distrust large government and any sort of welfare schemes. They are rock-ribbed Republicans.

While many do escape their family political culture, they are sometimes imprisoned in it by their own rebellion from it. Also, those family attitudes often linger on subliminally in their consciousness, affecting political choices.

## 2. *Regional Culture and History*

It would be extremely difficult to deny the continuing influence on Southern politics of that region's history and culture. Its Civil War history continues to color its attitude toward politics. Its history of racial relations continues to affect its politics. Its culture, deeply influenced by Southern evangelical religion, is a strong conditioner of political opinion. Regional influence is present in most other regions of the United States — the urban Northeast, the secular West, the Hispanic and retired-Anglo Southwest, the leisure-oriented Northwest, the Great Plains and Big Sky country, and the breadbasket Midwest. All exert a certain kind of influence on politics. If you are from Utah, for example, you are very likely to be a Republican; from Massachusetts a Democrat.

## 3. *National Culture and History*

It is amazing how differently Americans view political life than Europeans, or, for that matter, than their Canadian cousins. Americans honor individual self-reliance far more than their Canadian and European colleagues. They distrust government solutions more. They insist on more individual freedoms and rights. They support a more assertive role for their nation in the world. There are a host of cultural differences that make Americans distinct, many having to do with the historical experience of each national culture.

One peculiarity of American culture and history that is very relevant to politics is what has been called the "civil religion." Civil religion is the lowest-common-denominator religion of a country that has vibrant, diverse religious people and organizations but also has a law prohibiting the establishment of a particular church. Civil religion is what has been called the "deistic minimum," a shared commitment to concepts such as: God the Creator who has blessed and watched over America as well as judged it; God as final ground and guarantor of the values embedded in the Declaration of Independence and Constitution. The civil religion is the religion of the American Way.

It has its own holy days — Fourth of July, Memorial Day, Thanksgiving Day, Veterans Day, Constitution Day — as well as the rituals and liturgies that surround each. It has its own sacred texts — the Declaration and the Constitution — and "places of worship" — the Lincoln Memorial, the Washington Monument, the Capitol, as well as similar locations in the states. It offers a way to give transcendent meaning to the nation as well as to summon it to higher achievement. While most of its practitioners use it to put a religious gloss on the nation and its cause, the more profound employ it also to judge the nation and call it to a higher achievement of justice. When one reads Lincoln's Second Inaugural or listens to Martin Luther King Jr.'s "I Have a Dream" speech, one encounters that profound use of the civil religion.

While some of the Founding Fathers actually believed in the deistic minimum, the vast majority who have employed the civil religion are members of particular Christian communities. For them the civil religion is a shared set of meanings that can be effectively used to add religious meaning to the cause or activity they champion without getting into the specifics of a particular Christian denomination. When, for example, the nation experiences a traumatic event such as 9/11, the civil religion is employed to bring the nation together and to summon it to vigorous action. It also can be used to ponder the shortcomings of the nation that have led to the trauma. The civil religion can also be used to stir up the nation to enact public policy of high importance. When the Civil Rights Act of 1964 was enacted, it was accompanied by much high-blown civil religious rhetoric.

Many in specific religious communities have contempt for the civil religion because of its tendency to sponsor jingoistic nationalism, but that need not be the case. Operating from more specific religious traditions, wise practitioners can employ civil religious categories to bring both affirmation and critical scrutiny to the nation's policies, and to specific policies within the nation.

## 4. The Traditions of Western Civilization

Western civilization, deeply influenced by Christianity, has a powerful conditioning effect on all our thinking about politics. The West is where democratic practice and theory developed over many centuries. Those habits of mind and practice continue to shape its political way of life. Legal theory, theories of justice, and moral norms of both religious and philosophical provenance come into play as we try to shape policy. Above all, centuries of the history and experience of democracy shape our thinking about good and bad policy, about what we can expect of government and what we cannot. It is important to note that there are a plurality of normative schemes of justice and morality extant in the West. These competing notions of the good and the right certainly condition and complicate the process of moving from the Christian core to public policy.

These competing notions of the good and right issue in part from the effect of the Enlightenment on the Western tradition. The Enlightenment, in part reacting to warring religions and in part motivated by the rise of science and the recovery of classical learning, put forth the argument that humans have finally come of age, that is, they have been freed from the tutelage of religion and given tools of knowing that are far more reliable than those offered by religion. Reason and science became the ways of knowing that displaced those that relied on tradition and faith. Humans became autonomous — legislating morality and achieving knowledge through reason and science. With that sense of triumph, religion — and its intellectual companion, theology — were ushered to the margins of intellectual life. Indeed, for some radical versions of the Enlightenment religion was expunged from the public square entirely. The French banishment of religion from public life — *laïcité* — is a product of such a version.

Most inheritors of the Enlightenment vision tend to argue that religiously based arguments ought not to be used in the political sphere. (We have examined some of these arguments in Chapter Two.) They prefer "secular, public reason," which relies on what they believe are universal rational norms that all rational beings can recognize and articulate. They believe that "comprehensive schemes" borne by religions are too parochial and detailed — and possibly too dangerous — to be employed in political life. Thus, when religious people enter political life, they ought to leave these "comprehensive schemes" behind and argue according to more limited — yet more universal — canons of secular, rational morality. For example, if one is arguing for a public policy, it would be better to argue it on the basis of John Rawls's theory of justice than on a biblical notion of covenantal morality.

In this way, secular philosophy becomes a mediating or conditioning element as one moves from religious themes to public policy. For the more "separationist" of secular philosophers, the secular philosophy becomes a substitute for the religious themes. Indeed, for them there may be a total disconnect — the religious themes remain private while the secular philosophy is the sole tool used for public argument.

Our view is that it is often the case that secular moral philosophy can become a useful mediating instrument for moving from religiously based moral themes to public policy. Secular philosophy may add more specificity to the general religiously based moral themes if there is a strong affinity between those specific philosophical notions and the religious themes. Furthermore, employing secular philosophical language may appeal to more persons in the task of persuading them to support a particular public policy.

But the decision to use secular philosophical language is mainly a prudential one: What will be most effective in making the case for an argument that is essentially religiously based? Such an approach views such language as a mediating — and perhaps conditioning — instrument for moving from core to public policy. Using mediating language also protects religious themes from the danger of religion being fused with particular public policies, the kind of risk we talked about in Chapter Three. For these reasons, this approach is the prevalent one used by religious persons in the public sphere.

In some cases, however, it may be important to use direct religious arguments, especially if they overlap with the arguments other religious and philosophical traditions offer. Rarely, it may be the case that no other approach will be as effective or dramatic. When Martin Luther King Jr. wanted to appeal to Americans to expand civil rights to black citizens, he directly employed biblical themes and images. These allusions appealed to religious people, but also to the non-religious who resonate to civil religious themes.

However, there are no constitutional reasons why explicitly religious arguments cannot be used in the public sphere. All Americans — religious and secular alike — are guaranteed the right to exercise their religion, and that guarantee certainly applies to the exercise of religion in public. But that exercise should be limited by prudential considerations — to make a broader appeal or, perhaps more importantly, to protect religious themes from being co-opted and cheapened by political needs.

It should be added that these secular schemes of justice should be critically engaged from a Christian point of view. Some of them may have more affinity with key Christian moral themes than others; some may have little affinity and may have to be discarded. But, in any case, those theories need to be appropriated in a critical manner. Again, however, the process of engagement is complicated. Much depends on which Christian themes are accentuated and how those themes are ordered. One scheme of justice may be preferred by one Christian over another preferred by another Christian. Yet, not everything goes — it would be difficult for Christians to select schemes of justice that neglect the prospects of the least among us or that suppress basic rights.

### 5. Race, Class, Gender, and Marital Status

These categories could indeed stand on their own. Many political scientists are fixated on them as factors shaping political opinion, with good reason. Being black in America carries with it a specific history of solidarity with the Democratic Party that is difficult to resist. A small percentage of black conservatives do buck the tide, but often with punishing results, particularly if they are vocal. Class circumstances affect politics — the very poor do not participate politically, but those in precarious economic circumstances often opt for liberal politics. White males tend to be more Republican than Democrat, while white women edge a bit more toward liberalism. Single women and men tend toward the liberal spectrum of political opinion.

*6. Peer Group*

Certainly one of the most powerful influences on political attitudes is that exercised by peer groups at work, in the neighborhood, at church, or in friendship circles. Everyone wants to belong comfortably within the various social contexts in which they live their lives. Often these contexts have a definite political culture that is reinforced by the expectations of the group. Academic cultures are often pervasively liberal and assume that every member of intelligence and good intentions will follow the alleged consensus. It is difficult for conservatives to get a voice in such contexts, and they often remain quiet or leave. If they are vocal, they are often marginalized or forced out. Sometimes they are never hired because they do not fit the academic culture. Yet, academics believe that they are exceedingly tolerant and diverse. Academic cultures exhibit a wide gap between their rhetoric about themselves and the reality that they create.

Conservatives are no less immune to creating coercive peer cultures than liberals. Some churches enforce a political and cultural homogeneity that is stifling. Belonging has its dark side as well as its strong benefits. Contrary to the faddish endorsement of diversity we hear from almost every sector of society, people like to be with those with whom they feel comfortable, that is, they want to agree with their peer group on important matters, including politics. There is evidence that people more and more are gathering in like-minded enclaves. They read journals and newspapers that reinforce their opinions. They watch cable TV programs that do the same. They live in homogeneous neighborhoods. And they assume that everyone in their own social circle holds the same opinion on political issues. So peer-group pressure can be very strong in shaping political opinion. It can serve as a powerful conditioning factor as Christians move from their core beliefs to public policy options.

## 7. Religious Tradition and Intensity of Religious Practice

While we have already covered some conditioning factors that have been deeply influenced by religion, it is important to note that religion itself influences political commitments. That proposition, of course, is the central proposition of this book. Yet, there is merit in mentioning — without explaining how — that certain religious traditions lead in specific political directions. Judaism overwhelmingly correlates with political liberalism. While one could argue that what is at work in the Jewish commitment to liberalism is one of the conditioning factors already listed, that would pay disrespect to the genuine religious convictions that lead many Jews to political liberalism. The same would be true of the connection between evangelicals and conservative politics, between Catholics and liberalism in the past (though less so presently), and black religion and liberal politics. Mainstream Protestantism at the local level does not exhibit a strong affinity to either political party.

Interestingly enough, the intensity of religious practice seems to move people more toward the conservative camp. Even among those in liberal Protestantism, weekly attendance at services seems to move them more toward conservative political policies. Such is definitely true of highly observant Catholics, evangelicals, and Orthodox Jews. Conversely, the further persons are from practice of organized religion, the more likely they are to gravitate toward liberal policies. So, the intensity — or the lack thereof — seems to affect political preference.

Finally, it is also true that persons who belong to many groups with distinct political cultures are subject to cross-pressures. One group pushes them one way while another pulls them in yet a different direction. This reality also conditions the movement from core to periphery. Sometimes it may even paralyze that movement.

It should be mentioned that all of these conditioning factors, anchored in our finitude as human beings, are also exaggerated by the persisting sin of pride. The allure of nation or class or race or regional culture is not only the necessary stuff of life that gives us definition and place in life; it is also the occasion for exerting one's own pride in ways that lead to overweening self-interest and even oppression of one group by another. Given sinful pride, these conditioning elements can distort or even block out completely the Christian values that come from core Christian theological commitments. Christians, though never free from these conditioning factors, must be reflective about their sometimes-unconscious influence in political decision-making. Such critical engagement with these conditioning and mediating factors can help prevent Christians from simply adding a religious gloss to something that is not even religious. Such a use of religion then leads us back to an unconscious fusion of religion and politics on basically political terms, which leads to serious damage to religion's claims to a transcendent message.

## 8. Broad and Narrow Self-Interest

All the preceding factors figure into the broadly considered self-interest of Christians as they move from central convictions to public policy. Insofar as peer identification enters into their political preferences, for example, they are voting according to their self-interest broadly construed. But there is a narrower sense in which self-interest plays a powerful role, one that we can scarcely neglect. Indeed, some political theorists assume that everyone acts politically according to their narrow self-interest. While Christians cannot accept such an extreme theory, it is admittedly the case that their and their family's interests figure into their political preferences. And to some extent this is legitimate; everyone counts for one in the political process, and Christians and their own families should count. But this narrowly defined self-interest must be summoned out of its narrowness by Christian notions of love and justice, as well as the normative notions we have explored above. For Christians, self-interest may well be a conditioning factor, but it ought not be the only — or even the predominant — one.

## D. How, Then, Do We Proceed in Genuinely Engaging Religion and Politics?

It seems clear that the trajectory from core Christian theological beliefs to a specific public policy is a complex and jagged one. The process can be visualized by thinking of a circle with many concentric circles around it. In the center are the core theological beliefs we outlined at the beginning of the chapter. Those beliefs are the common ground for all Christians, and provide their crucial identity. They point to ultimate truth for believers, and serious Christians stake their lives upon that belief. Moreover, those central convictions do not change radically over time, though their articulation and interpretation must be re-done for every new generation. They are the treasure of the church, whose main mission it is to proclaim and teach them to the world. While there are nuances and distinctives belonging to each subtradition in the larger Christian tradition, the central convictions are widely shared. They are articulated succinctly in the Apostles' Creed. All sorts of Christians of every age and place gather around those central convictions — the Great Tradition. So there is unity at the center, with wide diversity and variety among those who hold to the center.[3]

The first concentric circle outward from the core corresponds to my earlier elaboration of "principles relevant to politics," in which I distilled three main principles from the whole corpus of Christian teaching that would be significant for politics. We could also designate this first circle the "social teachings" of the church. They are principles derived from the core that are addressed to challenges before the church. As the church faces challenges through time a body of social teaching is built up. Roman Catholic social teaching is the most instructive at this point. There is a whole body of teaching that the church has developed, drawing on the Bible and church tradition, and articulating those social teachings in sophisticated ar-

---

3. There are two faulty postures toward this center. One is that the formulations of the center are absolute and unchanging. Our view is that while the central truths have that character, the formulations of them — even the biblical account of them — are conditioned by human limitations. Therefore, there is a continuing struggle for clarity and coherence of belief, as well as room for the continued development of the meaning of those central truths. But that struggle is guided by the Holy Spirit working in and through the believing community that faithfully clings to the ongoing Great Tradition. The other faulty stance is the belief that the central convictions are so shaped by social settings, so distorted by hegemonic powers, and so time-bound that nothing can be taken as truth for us. We moderns can "liberate" ourselves from these distortions by approaching the tradition with suspicion and by insisting upon our own perspectival interpretation of the core. Thus, the meaning of the core is reduced to opinion, either the opinion of the ancient writers or that of the modern interpreter. In opposition to this, we maintain that genuine truth is mediated through the tradition. The human distortions of the tradition are small in comparison to the plenitude of what is genuinely and clearly communicated.

guments. For example, the social teaching on abortion is long-lived and extensive. Catholic consciences are to be formed by the social teachings of the church. Other churches have developed social teachings, but rarely as authoritative or as persuasive as those of the Roman Catholic Church. The Catholic Church's teachings do change over time, but very slowly. For example, for centuries the church had rejected "liberalism" — meaning market economics, social pluralism, religious freedom, and democratic politics. But slowly over the years the church has come critically to embrace them, owing much to the encyclicals of Pope John Paul II.

As can be seen, then, social and historical change does affect the social teachings. The "conditioning factors" I discussed earlier not only affect individuals, but also churches, as they try to move from core meanings to public policy. Indeed, it could be persuasively argued that the mainline Protestant churches and their ecumenical agencies (the World Council of Churches and the National Council of Churches) have been so heavily influenced by these conditioning factors that what they have endorsed as public policy is far more indebted to those conditioning factors (political culture of the elite, for example) than anything having to do with the core religious convictions. Of course, they try to justify their public policy choices by referring to biblical passages and theological themes, but they are highly selective in what they choose. They exhibit no persuasive argument for a necessary connection between core themes and public policy. And by constantly being swayed by the conditioning factors rather than solid social teachings, they are viewed more and more as one more interest group in the political fray. They suffer diminished support because they have shown more interest and zeal in their public policy commitments than they do in the communication of core theological beliefs. Moreover, their public policy commitments are unjustifiably partisan, oblivious to the complexity of moving from core to public policy.

The next concentric circle represents the application of relatively stable social teachings to new challenges that arise in the flux of historical life. For example, the United States and its allies decided that it was necessary to invade Iraq, depose Saddam Hussein, and try to establish a functioning democracy in that country that would be allied with the West. There are many factors to consider from the moral point of view in assessing the American invasion and ensuing warfare. Most Christians have at their disposal the "theory of just war" that has been in the Christian tradition since St. Augustine. They use that theory as a common starting point, assuming that it is consistent with the core commitments of the faith. However, while many theological ethicists come to the conclusion that the Iraq War was not justified by that theory, others claim it was. While most churches agree with the former conclusion, their laity exhibits no such uniformity. The movement from core to public policy, even when it draws upon common teaching such as the just war theory, does not move clearly to one public policy position. Room must be allowed for Christians of good will and intelligence to disagree.

The final circle is concrete public policy itself, which is the product for the most part of the executive and legislative branches of government. Good public policy is notoriously difficult to craft, because it often has unintended results that can produce just the opposite effects than what was intended. Public policy is also the product of much give and take, much compromise. Sometimes there are so many interests involved in the formation of the policy that it lacks coherence. Other times public policies are so encumbered by regulations that they become both baffling and grossly inefficient. Yet, it is necessary to forge public policy. This process is preeminently in the hands of politicians who have been elected by their constituencies, which adds another limiting factor in the shaping of public policy — the politicians have to be responsive to the interests of their constituencies.

Christian politicians are almost always laypersons. Even in the rare instances that they are clergy, they play the role of politician as a layperson. Indeed, Pope John Paul II thought the clash of callings between being a priest and a congressman was so severe that he required a Jesuit priest to resign from his political role. The best of politicians are able to master the process of public policy formation so that the policies they shape are not only effective, leading to the results intended, but also carry in them the moral values that are dear to the politician. So they employ principles derived from the Christian core, but in a very complex and variegated way.

Let's take, for example, two sets of major public policies in which Christians have been involved, one in which the trajectory from core to public policy seems clearer, another in which that trajectory is less clear. Each set contains a number of different kinds of policy that we will explore.

One cluster of policies in the first set is made up of what have been called "social issues." Policies that restrain abortion and policies that preserve the traditional notion of marriage come to mind. These seem to garner the most support by classical Catholics and conservative Protestants, and by those who are the most intensive Christians among the mainline Protestant denominations. Indeed, I would contend that this cluster exhibits one of the straighter — though it is far from straight — lines between core convictions and public policy. Take the restraint on abortion, for example. The Christian conviction that all humans are created in the image of God and all redeemed by the work of Christ leads to a strong affirmation of life even in its nascent forms. If a fertilized human egg is tended properly, it will result in a human life. All of us have been at that stage of development at one time. Ending that nascent life is certainly killing, even if such action may not rise to the level of murder. Further, the alleged "right to privacy" discovered in *Roe v. Wade* certainly ought not mean the unlimited right to kill developing life.

Christians rightly then support policies that require compelling reasons for abortion. But even here prudential considerations intervene. Does damage to the "health" of the mother constitute a serious reason to abort a fetus, or should that reason be elevated to danger to the life of the mother? Should pregnancies caused by rape or incest fall under the category of compelling reasons? How about seriously deformed fetuses? More poignantly, how about Down Syndrome babies? Further, do too-restrictive policies simply push the abortion enterprise underground, with grave dangers to women? Are women to be forced to bring an unwanted pregnancy to term, even if they are adamant in their refusal? What sanctions should apply to those who have abortions for frivolous reasons? What incentives and disincentives are possible to embed in policies so that reverence for life is enhanced?

Nevertheless, even with all these considerations, the pressure of core Christian belief pushes Christians toward policies that restrain abortion. That core belief leads large majorities of Christians to reject procedures such as "partial birth abortion" as well as legislation such as the Freedom of Choice Act, which, if enacted, would sweep away all the restraints against abortion enacted by the states and the federal government in the last thirty years.

The same sort of pressure leads Christians to support policies that uphold classical views of marriage. Not only has the long history of Christian moral teaching decisively and rightfully shaped Western ideas and laws concerning marriage, but there are compelling secular reasons for limiting marriage to a life-long covenantal relation between one man and one woman. That arrangement seems by far the best for bringing children into the world and nurturing them for the common good. Given that, it seems a fairly straightforward move to support such a social arrangement through public policy. Christians exhibit more disagreement over public policy that allows civil unions for gays and lesbians.

Another cluster of issues in which a relatively straight line can be drawn from the core to public policy is that surrounding a "safety net" for the most vulnerable in our society, particularly children but also those who through no fault of their own cannot provide for themselves — those whose mental and physical deficiencies are so severe that they are completely dependent on others, for example. Or, to list another example, those soldiers who have been severely injured in the two wars America has been fighting. When men and women in the armed forces experience serious losses in their efforts to serve their country, public policy ought to provide the best of medical service and care for them. Christian commitment to justice certainly presses Christians to care for the least and last through governmental means. Public policy becomes much more difficult to construct when it is directed to a safety net for those who are able to work.

Even these relatively straight-line trajectories do not lead necessarily to specific public policies, because each public policy has to be scrutinized not only from a Christian ethical point of view but also from prudential points of view: Will it benefit the persons it is supposed to benefit? Is it needlessly cumbersome? Will it have unexpected results? Is it as efficient as possible, is it feasible, and is it passable? So, in Christian critical engagement with specific policies, there is much room for practical disagreement and negotiation. Yet, those core commitments definitely press in a specific direction.

A final cluster of issues upon which Christians ought to find wide agreement among themselves regards the protection of religious liberty at home and abroad. The most important relation that people have — their relation to God — ought not be coerced. The first freedom that all peoples should enjoy is religious freedom, not only the freedom to worship as they choose but also the freedom to exercise their religion privately and publicly. There are limits, of course, to religiously based behavior when it clashes with the settled moral convictions of a country and its laws, but the latitude for such freedom ought to be wide indeed.

On the other side of the ledger, there are negative policies that do not jibe with any line from the core to public policy. There are cases in which public policy is so out of line with core Christian moral commitments that Christians just have to say "no." There is little room for negotiation. No line of congruence can be drawn from the core to public policy. For example, German Christians in the Nazi era ought to have been able simply to say "no" to Hitler's genocidal policies. Or, as an example from the same era, the Norwegian Bishop Berggrav simply said "no" to a Nazi policy that required the church to accede to anti-Jewish actions. Many American Christians found it fitting simply to say "no" to policies that required segregation of the races. More recently, most Christians in the world said "no" to the Apartheid policies in South Africa even though they disagreed about how to attack them. Many contemporary Christians think the same way about policies such as the Freedom of Choice Act, which would sweep away any limits on abortion.

Now to the other set of public policies, those in which the steps between core and policy are so fraught with disagreement that clear connections are impossible. A whole range of public policy issues — perhaps the vast majority of them — exhibit a tangled journey from core to policy. There simply are too many steps in the movement from core to public policy, involving too many prudential judgments, to construct anything like a straight line. Foreign policy concerning Iraq is one such policy.

What to do about the economic recession is another. So are proposed policies about what to do with regard to global warming. Many more could be listed.

Does this mean there is no room for critical engagement, that the trajectory from core to public policy is so muddled that there can be little occasion for Christian ethical grappling with a host of public policy options? No, it doesn't. As long as there is some moral component to policy, which is almost always the case, there is room for critical engagement. But because the Christian theological and ethical vision is so developed and complex, many different ethical themes can be employed in engaging specific political challenges, and each political actor may pick a different set of themes. Moreover, those themes may be ordered and interpreted in very different ways by each actor. So, for example, Christians can draw upon Christian themes to defend the use of market mechanisms in forging public policy, just as other Christians can draw upon other themes to defend governmental intervention. It would be far more difficult, if not impossible, to find themes that would legitimate totalitarian political arrangements. But even given the broad range of themes that could legitimate both market and interventionist arrangements, there would also be ethical norms that would severely challenge both arrangements. How do they treat the most vulnerable? How do they protect and encourage the freedom and dignity of persons? How do they promote the common good? How do they make it possible for the church to work freely?

The answers to those questions are not simple or clear, but the questions themselves are very important, and just the kind of questions Christians should ask of public policy, in addition to the more prudential concerns we raised above. Both sets of questions are involved in the Christian critical engagement with public policy. It is more important that Christians ask those questions of every policy than for them to make premature commitment to specific policies, though finally legislators must opt for a particular policy.

## Conclusion

For Christian individuals and for Christian churches there is no question that their core convictions must and will be exercised in their quest for discerning and promoting good public policies. Those core convictions are indeed exercised. But while those core convictions are necessary for Christians, they are not sufficient. There are many other necessary factors that go into the making of good choices in public policy in almost all cases. There are many opportunities for critical engagement all along the trajectory from core to policy. Yet, there are some consistent directions toward which those core convictions lead. We have indicated some of those. Now it is necessary to reflect on the practical ways that such convictions reach the public sphere of policy.

*Chapter Five*

# The Practical Engagement
# of Religion and Politics

By now it must be clear that religion does in fact and ought to engage politics. (Politics likewise engages religion, but that is another subject.) However, we have argued that the engagement is anything but simple or unequivocal. While religion does and ought to lead in some definite directions, it ought generally to avoid identification with specific public policies, political parties, or ideologies. Engagement, yes; straight-line connection, no.

Thus far, though, we have not addressed the intensely practical question of "how" religion engages with politics. We have rather reflected on the theoretical questions concerning whether and how religion and politics ought to interact. Now is the time to grapple with nitty-gritty practical issues. The practical "how" question inquires into the manner of engagement — indirectly through individuals and voluntary associations or directly through the institutional church's influence and action.

For the purposes of keeping our discussion as manageable as possible, let us assume that we are dealing with organized religious traditions, not merely religious individuals. The latter are far too amorphous and varied to deal with in this approach. That is, let us assume that ongoing religious communities have adherents who are so deeply shaped and formed by those religious communities that it is likely that authentic religious ideas and values would be expressed in the public lives of adherents of those communities. Likewise, let us assume that those religious communities are organized enough to be institutional players in the political game itself, and that they have theologies that require them to engage in that game in some way.

I will present a typology of four ways that such religion affects politics, moving from the non-controversial and low-profile to the highly controversial and high-profile kinds of engagement. The first two types are what I call "indirect" modes — those in which the religious community or church does not involve itself institutionally in political decision-making. It does not itself become a political actor. Rather, its connection to politics is indirect, through its laity as individuals or its laity banded together in faith-based voluntary associations. The latter two types are what I call "direct" — those in which the church as institution tries to persuade or pressure political actors to enact or reject specific policies.

The first indirect way of engaging politics is one in which the religious tradition does not even intend to affect political life. This mode is called *indirect* and *unintentional influence*. I have already indicated what is meant by indirect. By unintentional I mean that the church has no conscious intent to affect policy, and it has no specific blueprint toward which it wants to move society. Influence means that the church relies on persuasion, first that of its own members and then later by its own members acting in political life.

### The Ethics of Character

This "indirect and unintentional influence" might also be termed *the ethics of character.* When the church really exists as a living tradition, it shapes people — their outlook, their virtues, and their moral values. When the church is really the church, its preaching, teaching, worship, and discipline form and sometimes transform persons so that their innermost being is powerfully shaped. Persons become deeply affected by the biblical and theological narrative we sketched at the beginning of Chapter Four, as well as the relevant political principles and ethic of Christian service we sketched there.

Affecting people in this way is arguably the most important, fundamental, and potentially most effective way the church influences political life. There have been many historical studies tracing this kind of indirect and unintentional influence. One of the most celebrated is Max Weber's *The Protestant Ethic and the Spirit of Capitalism,* in which Weber argues that Reformed piety of a certain sort, which he calls "inner worldly asceticism," was crucial in the development of Western capitalism. Those Calvinists were not intentionally effecting a new economic order, nor were they acting coercively as a religious institution to effect that order. But they were pervasively forming persons, who then acted in ways that energized a nascent capitalism.

In a more political vein, Alfred Lord Lindsay, in his *Essentials of Democracy,* maintains that Reformation doctrines of the equality of all sinners before God's judgment and grace worked through the governance practices of English non-conformist sects and gradually surfaced to encourage democratic political ideas and practices in the public sphere. The non-conformist religious tradition had no intention of shaping secular politics, but it did, indirectly and unintentionally.

The point in these illustrations is that religious communities are capable of forming a powerful ethos among people who participate. These people then shape the world about them, as voters and political leaders. Who can doubt that the ethos of "biblical virtue," to use the language of Robert Bellah in his *Habits of the Heart,* has decisively shaped many of our voters and leaders? True enough, the conditioning factors we mentioned earlier also operate to shape people, but the religious ethos certainly does its share. For instance, the ethos that shaped Mike Huckabee and the voters who supported him was deeply anchored in Southern evangelicalism.

There are many other political leaders who have been deeply informed by their religious traditions; some are more overt and recognizable than others. Catholic political figures such as Henry Hyde on the conservative side and Ted Kennedy on the liberal side both draw upon Catholic Christian themes. Lutherans such as Paul Simon on the liberal side and Edwin Meese on the conservative draw upon Lutheran Christian themes. Evangelicals such as Jimmy Carter on the one hand and Sarah Palin on the other are decisively shaped by their traditions. One could also add those coming from Presbyterian, Episcopal, Jewish, and Mormon traditions. The number of people in politics whose faith is a crucial motivating and guiding factor for them is legion.

This indirect and mostly unintentional mode of affecting politics is quite widespread even though it is often not very visible. Certainly this mode is an inevitable part of serious religion and constitutionally guaranteed. Moreover, short of the invention of some sort of thought control, this mode could not possibly be suppressed, even by totalitarian regimes. Some practitioners of this mode try to keep their religious identities muted while others are not shy about claiming their identities publicly. The latter sometimes elicit protestations that they are violating the principle of the separation of church and state, but that is clearly bogus. They are simply operating out of their deepest convictions, though they must be vigilant in not crassly using their religious identity for political purposes.

When this mode becomes active and visible in candidates, voters of sincere religious persuasion are attracted to those candidates. Thus, intensely religious people tend to identify with and vote for others who have been shaped by a similar religious ethos. They believe that political leaders who are evangelicals similar to themselves are deeply affected by the Christian narrative, by the political values we elaborated above, and by the ethic of Christian service. They have strong affinities with them. If they are wise, those same voters make assessments about whether the candidate has the requisite secular or non-moral virtues that are necessary for political life, as well as the common moral virtues that public-spirited citizens should have. Further, they should pay close attention to the policy propensities of the candidates. Given positive assessments about these, though, serious observant Christians often give support to candidates who share their Christian worldview, values, and policy preferences, the Christian virtues of faith, love, and hope, and the Christian sense of vocation that all Christians should manifest. Insofar as those features are present, there is a strong and understandable attraction then between the voter and the Christian politician.

Thus, it is not surprising that observant conservative practitioners of Christianity of all traditions tend to support observant conservative Christian political figures who share their beliefs and values, but also share their commitment to pro-life policies as well as their support for policies that affirm traditional marriage. As I mentioned above, such policies seem to be connected to core Christian convictions in a straighter line than most. Thus, intense religion is definitely related to specific conservative policies, and justly so.

Sometimes assessments of religious candidates by religious voters become too refined. Instead of making broad judgments about their Christian outlook and values, they apply finely tuned theological criteria to the candidate, which seems out of place in the political sphere. For example, it seems that many evangelicals did not support Mitt Romney in his bid for the presidency because they did not consider him to be an orthodox Christian. Such theological distinctions, though important in churchly affairs, seem largely irrelevant in political life where general religious and moral virtues and political programs should hold sway. We elect politicians, not pastors or theologians.

Committed liberal Christians are likely to support politicians and policies that offer support for the most vulnerable children (already living!) in our society, particularly programs and policies such as CHIP (Children's Health Insurance Program) and WIC (Women, Infants, Children — a federal program that gives grants to states for providing adequate nutrition to poor women, infants, and children). While many conservative Christians also support such policies and the politicians who promote them, conservatives are more likely than liberals to give time and money to independent, voluntary organizations that offer help to the poor. But it would seem that all Christians — both liberal and conservative — should give support to policies that help the most vulnerable. Likewise, it would seem that all Christians — both liberal and conservative — should support policies that restrain abortion. The lines from core commitments to specific policies are straighter than most with regard to these two sets of issues, and both should draw the support of Christian politicians and voters. Core Christian commitments should reliably lead well-formed Christians in their direction.

Although this type of indirect and unintentional influence is still very obvious in many Western lands, it is less telling in European cultures. There the churches are losing their capacity for character formation simply because few people participate in them actively. It is one of my notions that the eruption of youthful working-class violence in England is linked to the collapse of non-conformist Christianity in England. While the Church of England has experienced a serious erosion in participation, the

Reformed, Congregational, and Methodist churches have declined even more. These were the churches that once evangelized and formed working-class people.

Americans, however, should not be smug. The character-shaping capacity of the churches, especially the mainline churches, is waning. Biblical virtue is in sharp competition with other visions of life, and the churches are not serious and intentional enough about deeply imprinting their members, particularly the young, so that they can keep the faith in the hard challenges ahead. The story is somewhat different for evangelicals, fundamentalists, Mormons, and conservative Catholics.

There is an irony connected with this first type that I cannot help but note. It has to do with the relation of the first indirect mode to the more direct approaches I will discuss later, in which the church as an institution becomes a visible public actor. Historically, it seems that when the churches were able to instill their vision and values in members they were relatively quiescent as public actors. Now, when particularly the mainstream Protestant churches and the Catholic Church are less able and willing to form their members morally and spiritually, those churches put heavier emphasis on their role as public actors. A nasty observer might note that when the churches can no longer persuade their own people they make greater attempts to get their way politically through more coercive means.

Many persons in church and society would like to limit the relation of religion and politics to this indirect and unintentional mode. It is low profile and generally non-controversial; even tyrannical regimes don't bother churches if they stick to this approach. Moreover, this approach, if fueled by effective religious communities, has a far-reaching and long-term effect on political life. Who would rather have a plethora of church statements instead of strong believers in public positions? Many laypeople, perhaps a majority, believe that if the church really does its job of character formation well, that is all it need do. The church would do its job and then set the laity free to do theirs.

However, most Christians — including this writer — are not satisfied with this mode as the only way in which organized religion affects the political realm. Its indirectness forces laity to make all the connections between religion and politics, a task that we know is often not done particularly well. Laypeople sometimes dichotomize their religious and political lives. They also often let conditioning factors smother the religious. Further, its lack of intentionality reduces the witness of the church to spontaneous, often unconscious, connections. It is too long-term, general, and unpredictable. It is fine and good to plant oak trees, but we also need to plant a few pumpkins, which not only grow more rapidly but yield the fruits of our efforts in a more direct and tangible way. In short, sole reliance on this mode is incomplete.

## The Ethics of Conscience

The key difference between the first and this second type of religion-politics connection has to do with the element of intentionality. Organized religion in this mode directs its moral teaching self-consciously to specific issues in the public sphere. It matches up specific teaching with specific issues. Yet, the church's connection to politics remains indirect through its laity; it is not primarily a public actor. It aims to form the conscience of its own people regarding public issues by bringing its moral traditions to bear on these specific items.

The church begins with relevant biblical texts and themes, works through the theological modulations of those texts and themes, draws upon secular philosophical and social-scientific perspectives, and articulates its social teachings. It tries to relate all of that to the pressing issues at hand in a self-conscious reflective way *within* the institution. The church does not make public statements purporting to represent the members of that community. Rather, it aims at inculcating its social teachings in its people, forming a common conscience on the principles, aims, and ends of those teachings. It does not allow them to float above the thorny political issues, but rather encourages a lively interaction between its social teachings and contemporary public challenges. At the same time, it assumes a variety of political persuasions within the church and therefore supports open discussion of the means by which those principles and ends might be achieved.

The teaching involved in this mode can happen in a number of different places — from the pulpit, in adult forums, Sunday School classes, study groups, colleges or universities associated with specific religious traditions, or through materials developed by churches that are disseminated to their members. Sometimes the teaching does not involve endorsements of particular policies in the light of that teaching, but sometimes it does. The latter can be quite controversial within churches, and should generally be accompanied by opportunities for open discussion of the endorsement. Laypersons do not like to be "told what to do," especially if it is too specific.

Let me give examples of both approaches. After our government launched the invasion of Iraq in 2003, our local congregation provided a series of adult forums on Christian perspectives on the use of violence. I taught the variety of perspectives on the justification of the use of lethal force in Christian history, running from the pacifist position to "crusader" ethics. However, I argued that the great mainstream Christian traditions — Catholic, Reformed, Lutheran — all accepted "just war theory." Since we were Lutherans I showed how Martin Luther taught out of that perspective, justifying Christian participation in a just war. I outlined the seven or eight principles that belong to the contemporary version of the theory, and explained how they might or might not justify our invasion of Iraq.

The next Sunday a layperson who believed that the invasion was justified held forth. He argued that the reasons for going to war fit the criteria of the just war theory and therefore supported the Bush administration's policy. The next Sunday a layperson argued that the invasion could not be justified by the same criteria. A further Sunday was devoted to an open discussion led by a panel made up of the speakers from the earlier sessions.

In another congregation the pastors consistently observe "pro-life Sunday" and preach on texts that assert the sacrality of life from the womb onward. In the run-up to the election of 2008, the pastors not only preached on those texts but outlined the consistent position Christians have taken throughout history against abortion. They also cited the "pro-life" themes in the social statement of the Evangelical Lutheran Church in America. They stopped short of endorsing a candidate by name, but the implication was clear that one candidate — John McCain — had a more consistent history of resisting abortion than Barack Obama. A number of parishioners reacted angrily to the messages that came from the pulpit, claiming that the pastors were telling them how to vote and that those who believe in abortion rights were made to feel that they were not fully Christian. But most of the congregation did not react negatively. They were free to accept or not accept the teaching from the pulpit, or to balance the issue of abortion with other issues they were concerned about.

In the same election there were propositions or state constitutional amendments put before the electorate in a number of states that defined marriage in the traditional sense. Many pastors drew upon Christian arguments for marriage being defined as a lifelong covenant between one man and one woman, which in turn they saw as the basic building block of society and the best arrangement for the care and nurture of children. They believed that courts would overturn that traditional definition unless it were enacted in the constitution of the state. Evidently the preaching and teaching in the churches were quite effective. Laypersons connected traditional Christian social teaching with the proposition before them and acted upon their convictions. Even in liberal California the proposition passed.

Sometimes churches as institutions took positions on these matters, going beyond the indirect mode. But the examples I have given above do not assume that. What they do assume is that churches have moral teachings that can be brought to bear on the issues of the day, and they bring that interaction before the laity in order to stimulate and form consciences. It seems preferable in most cases to allow and encourage debate among members on the various policies that would best fit those teachings. That gives room both for disagreement and for the stimulation of critical thought on the part of Christian laypersons. At the same time it presses the laity to connect their religious convictions with political issues in the larger world.

Finally, there is a very important kind of indirect religious engagement with politics that is something of a combination of the unintentional and the intentional. As churches form the character (unintentional) and consciences (intentional) of their laity, those laypeople often organize faith-based voluntary associations that vigorously express religious moral convictions in the political sphere. In the case of ethics of character, the moral values of the religious tradition are so deeply embedded in the laity that they — without any direction from the leadership of the organized tradition — experience a great desire to act upon those values politically and socially. They then either organize or join such faith-based organizations.

On the other hand, when churches employ the ethics of conscience, they intentionally connect religiously based moral teachings with the issues of the day. They encourage those members who are "conscientiousized" to form or join politically oriented faith-based organizations. They know that the membership of their churches are a diverse lot politically, and the churches themselves cannot become directly active politically without fracturing the membership. In many cases they also ought not become directly active. So, independent associations take up the political task. Sometimes clergy become leaders of the voluntary associations, but not in their roles as parish pastors. More often the associations are lay led and can vigorously express controversial political agendas without endangering the unity of the church or the integrity of the cause.

It should be mentioned that the vast majority of faith-based voluntary associations spun off either unintentionally or intentionally by the church are devoted to non-political ends. Social, athletic, recreational, educational, support, and especially charity organizations are much more common than politically oriented ones. And this is as it should be, since the church is devoted to many more purposes than merely political. "Service" organizations are a likely spin-off of effective churches.

It is stunning how many independent, cause-oriented, faith-based organizations are generated by each Christian church tradition. It is even more impressive how many faith-based organizations are ecumenical in nature. These associations take up political tasks the church cannot take up because the church's mission simply cannot be defined in such a directly political fashion. The associations provide distance from the churches so that the church's message can address all people, not just the ones partisan to this or that political cause.

A list from just the Lutheran tradition illustrates the point. *Lutherans for Life* advocates both internally within the churches and externally for pro-life causes. *Lutherans Concerned* does the same for gay/lesbian causes, as does *Lutheran Peace Fellowship* for war and peace issues. Other independent advocacy organizations could be listed here: *Lutheran Human Relations Association* on justice issues; *Alternatives for Simple Living* on ecological issues; *Evangelical Lutheran Educational Association* on educational issues. Many more ecumenical associations provide political outlets for energized Lutheran laity to express their moral and religious values. *Bread for the World, Interfaith Worker Justice, Amnesty International, Ecumenical Eco-Justice Network, Ecumenical Advocacy Days, Children's Defense Fund, Jubilee USA, Right to Life,* and the *Christian Coalition* are but a few. The list could be expanded indefinitely, and that would not include the many faith-based independent associations spawned by specific churches. Associations spawned unintentionally and intentionally by the Catholic Church would expand the list enormously.

Each one of these organizations makes its own movement from core convictions through the intervening steps — including the conditioning factors — to specific policies with passion and confidence. Other organizations from the same religious tradition may make a different journey to competing policy positions. But this illustrates well that there are many moral themes in the Christian tradition and that well-informed and well-intentioned Christians can make different judgments as they move from core to policy. Certainly some journeys are more accurate and compelling than others, but in a free society where Christians make different judgments it is good that they can do so. But it is also good that the commitment to specific policies is done by independent voluntary associations, not by the church. Identifying the church too closely with such specific policies will make it one more interest group in the contest for political influence and power, and undermine its capacity to bring a universal message to all sinners, no matter what side of the political faultline they find themselves.

A majority of persons in church and society would like to limit

93

the role of religion in politics to these indirect modes, particularly when they include the political roles of independent, faith-based, voluntary associations. The indirect modes have many positive attributes — they do not involve churches that claim to have a universal message in partisan politics; they avoid the usurpation of lay roles in politics by clergy or religious institutions; they do not violate laws separating church and state; and they divert bitter controversy and divisiveness away from the church toward persons and associations who can better bear them.

Hopefully, this kind of intentional and indirect influence will gain more acceptance in American churches. There is a great need and challenge for the churches to play a mediating role by providing the context for serious discussion of permissible Christian options on political issues. Conscience can be formed without the churches hastening to premature commitments to specific policy positions.

## Direct Modes

Yet, these two kinds of indirect modes — unintentional and intentional — are insufficient. There are occasions when the church as church must involve itself directly in political issues. The church is a corporate body with a coherent identity and vision; it is more than its deployed laity. And it is charged with articulating God's law to the world directly, which brings us to the two kinds of direct involvement.

They are direct in the sense that churches as institutions become involved in the political process. However, the direct mode breaks into two further forms — one that uses persuasion as its method and one that uses more coercive means of pressing its case. The first can be called "the church as social conscience" and the second "the church with power." Both modes are far more controversial than those that are indirect. People notice that the church as an institution is taking a position that often is contested. They — especially if they are members of the church taking the position — get upset if the position taken is different from their own. If the church takes positions on too many issues of public policy, citizens begin to think that the church acts primarily as a political rather than a religious institution. They begin to believe it is driven by political ideology rather than theology. Further, too many interventions suggest that the church has special competency in these worldly matters, which to most it patently does not. The upshot of too many such interventions is that the church is reduced to just another interest group in the eyes of citizens.[1] That is why majorities of Americans — church people and secular people — disapprove of ecclesial bodies and their leaders giving public advice to their political representatives.

---

1. The liberal Protestant churches — and their ecumenical agencies, the National Council of Churches and the World Council of Churches — have identified themselves so consistently with liberal policies that they can no longer gain sufficient support from their member churches to sustain themselves. They are pale shadows of their former selves. The laity of those supporting churches and many persons on the outside view the leadership of those churches and their ecumenical agencies as politically partisan agencies worthy of little respect as religious institutions. They have allowed the "conditioning factor" of liberal political ideology to play the determinative role in moving from core to policy. Yet, they claim to be speaking unequivocally from Christian principles and allow little room for disagreement among their various constituencies. Further, they do not heed the gap between the unanimity of their voices as leaders of liberal Protestantism and the pluralism of political opinion of their grassroots membership. Real political leaders, of course, do see that gap and therefore give little heed to what is proposed. In recent years, as conservative churches such as the Southern Baptist Church have found their political voice, they too have spoken too often according to conservative political ideology, and thereby have come to be looked upon as instruments of political conservatism. One difference, however, is that their members tend to be in more agreement with their leadership than is the case with the liberal Protestant churches. All these politically active churches need to be far more reticent in their direct speaking to the political sphere.

## The Church as Social Conscience

Why, then, propose a role for the church as social conscience? Mainly because the church is the bearer of the Christian moral and intellectual tradition and is called upon to engage the world with that tradition. Put more theologically, the church is the bearer of the Word of God as both Law and Gospel and, since God is creator and sovereign sustainer of the world, the church is obligated to hold that world up to the mirror of God's Law. The church indeed has a prophetic role. It must hold political life accountable in some fashion to God's commandments.

A prophetic role the church is most obviously obligated to play is to say "no" to political ideologies and policies that clearly violate its core convictions. It is even more genuinely prophetic when it refuses to bow to those ideologies and policies in its own practices. There are many historical examples of such a prophetic role. A very famous one is when the Nazi regime — with some success — tried to press its racist ideology onto the Christian churches in Germany. The Barmen Declaration, articulated and supported by Christians who would not compromise fundamental Christian belief, declared that the state cannot interfere with the integrity of the church's essential beliefs. Further, it declared that such ideologies contradicted Christian doctrines about the dignity of all human life. Other churches resisted the Nazis by saying "no" to such policies. Pope Pius XII denounced the Nazi stance and actions toward Jews. The brave Lutheran Norwegian Bishop Berggrav not only said "no" to Nazi interference in the church but resisted it. When the Nazis demanded that policies against the Jews be announced in the Lutheran churches of Norway, Berggrav commanded his pastors not to do so and not to cooperate in any way with the Nazis.

Similar examples of saying "no" occurred in the years of Apartheid in South Africa. Many churches said "no" to such policies; some even pronouncing the ideology and practice of Apartheid as an occasion for *status confessionis,* that is, an issue in which the faith itself is at stake. The very integrity of the faith is threatened by those who inside and outside the church believe in and practice such policies.

However, once the "no" was said it was far less clear what to do then. After the Nazis consolidated totalitarian power, churches were soon silenced, but their laypeople, whose consciences were formed in the churches, took many different paths. The following examples would fit under our "indirect" modes of political action by Christians. Some Christians participated in underground resistance. A small group plotted an attack on Hitler's life. A number of German politicians — such as Carl Gördeler, Mayor of Leipzig — participated in political resistance to the Nazi regime. Some wrote enough attacks on Nazi policies that they were expelled. Others were muzzled and put under house arrest. Yet others privately disagreed but were silent in the public sphere. Many claimed ignorance about what was happening and were obedient to the Nazi state. Some fled. One can no doubt locate authentic Christians among all these options. We honor those who risked their lives in resistance, but that was relatively few. It would be difficult to impute moral turpitude to those who took less heroic routes. Even those who complied with Nazi policies — soldiers, for example — could be anguished Christians.

Outside Germany, many churches spoke out against the Nazi regime, though debates remain about whether they were robust enough in speaking out. It has been hotly contested over many years whether Pope Pious XII spoke and acted decisively enough.

A similar set of challenges arose in the struggle against Apartheid. The most difficult decisions, of course, took place within South Africa, where churches paid a real price for continuing to say "no." The price, of course, was not nearly as high for those churches as for those under Nazism. Yet, it took courage for churches to speak out and even more to take action. Churches abroad that denounced Apartheid adopted a number of strategies. Some were content simply to denounce it but others took direct action, running from selective divestment from corporations doing business in South Africa to total divestment. These strategies fall into our next category of "direct action," since they involve the exercise of coercive power. Direct action, as we shall see, generally touches off serious conflict within the churches that participate in it.

Another very important mode of "direct influence" is for churches dramatically to call attention to grave injustices or compelling needs in the society, and then call for public policies to address those issues. This is an obvious way that the church can exercise its role as "social conscience." For example, the churches have repeatedly called attention to the disturbing number of people in our society who have no health insurance coverage. Catholic and evangelical churches have called attention to the roughly 1.3 million abortions performed each year in this country. Many denominations have lamented the poor quality of urban education. Conservative churches have called attention to the level of sex and violence in popular entertainment. The hunger campaigns of many denominations point to the number of hungry people in the world, often focusing on the number of children who die every day from disease and starvation.

The churches not only call attention to these issues in their statements, but in many cases take action on them themselves through various church agencies. In so doing they act as "social pioneers," providing models of just and charitable treatment of the lost, the last, and the least. This is a particularly important means of persuasion. When churches sense a problem and then respond to it well within their own body, they model to the world effective ways to address pressing issues. The church has had a long history of such "pioneering," sensing the need for hospitals, universities, orphanages, homes for the elderly, kindergartens, day care centers, hospices, urban renewal programs, elementary and secondary schools, food pantries, world hunger programs, and pre-school programs. Often the surrounding society then perceives that the church cannot reach everyone through these agencies, and organizes its own, sometimes imitating and perhaps improving on the churches' work. Thus, the church effectively persuades the world to act upon the needs it has pointed out for itself and the society. Recently, the American government has moved toward developing ways of helping to fund faith-based ministries of this sort. While that is to be applauded in many ways, the churches must be careful that the special character of their service is not undermined by government requirements and regulations.

A sad fact is that many of the service institutions pioneered by the church have become too expensive for the church to own and run. Hospitals are a good example. Some of the displacement of the church by publicly funded institutions is fitting, but the church should try to maintain shining models of these institutions to indicate just how the churches can contribute to human flourishing in ways that the secular society cannot do. Thus, the church should focus on a small number of high-quality institutions in each of these categories so that it might always provide quality models for how such services might be done. Moreover, it will add its particular religious contributions to such services, something that is often impossible among public agencies.

Another sad fact is that many of these pioneering agencies — social service, educational, charitable — have survived and flourished by becoming dependent on funding from far beyond their own constituencies, and in the process have lost their own religious "soul." They have been professionalized, specialized, and secularized, all in one seamless process. In due time there is little to warrant a continuing connection to a church, and many of them do the honest thing and sever those ties. Others maintain a gentle hypocrisy by claiming to have a meaningful connection when in fact none really exists. The most committed church-related institutions, however, are able to maintain both quality and soul by insisting on the continuing public relevance of their sponsoring religious tradition to all facets of their organizational lives. One hopes for the continuing presence of those robust agencies, for they are truly the ones who embody a religious vision of human flourishing that can provide a persuasive beacon for the surrounding society.

By saying "no," by non-cooperation and resistance in its own life, by dramatically calling attention to grave issues of neglect or injustice, and by pioneering efforts to address looming issues in their surrounding societies, churches have acted as the social conscience of many earthly cities. Yet, churches do not seem satisfied with that panoply of avenues. They want to make social statements about the general direction public policy should take, sometimes even opting for specific policies. Often they do this on the basis of social statements churches have made about particular issues, but sometimes leaders of the churches — bishops, presidents, advocates — make statements favoring or disfavoring specific public policy options.

Some churches are very parsimonious about their public utterances. The Lutheran Church–Missouri Synod, for example, speaks only for policies that limit the practice of abortion and against policies that encourage it. In addition, that church has a long history of publicly guarding religious freedom. Its early history in this country was fraught with fears that state governments would prohibit private religious schools, something to which it has always been committed. So it guards its freedom to educate its young, and in so doing helps to protect other forms of religious exercise.

Other churches are not so abstemious. Every mainline Protestant church seems to have agencies that claim to provide specific direction for the political sphere. Indeed, some of them have statements on scores of issues. Most remain at a level of high generality, but often their recommendations push in very specific directions. These statements are meant to convey the church's thinking on areas of public responsibility to its laity, who then are awakened to issues and given help in making up their minds. Further, the statements are meant to persuade the general public as well as political figures, though it is highly unlikely that many Protestant statements make much of an impact on those targets. Finally, they are meant to become the bases for advocacy efforts in the churches' state and federal advocacy offices. We will discuss "advocacy" in the next section.

My church, the Evangelical Lutheran Church in America, is a mainline Protestant church that is prolific in its public pronouncements, in harmony with its declaration that it is now a "public church." Statements, messages, and pronouncements come from many sources — task forces assembled to address specific social issues; the church council; and especially its presiding Bishop. The Bishop makes many, many public pronouncements, ostensibly hoping to persuade both the church's laypeople and the public authorities of the wisdom of his offerings.

Since its inception in 1987, the ELCA has made full-blown social statements (written by task forces and affirmed by a churchwide assembly) on abortion, the church's role in society, the death penalty, economic life, education, environment, health and health care, peace, and race, ethnicity, and culture. In all this, the church aims to "bring God's justice not only in the world but also in the church." It has just (2009) made a statement on human sexuality and will be making statements on genetics and criminal justice. It has many more "messages" — adopted by the ELCA Church Council — that are purportedly built on the social statements of the church. Some of these are "social policy actions," which get very specific. Many have to do with the conflict between Israel and the Palestinians. Among these social policy actions are a number that demand an immediate end to building the wall between Israel and the West Bank and call for an end to the "occupation" of Palestinian territories. Indeed, the ELCA has a whole strategy called "Peace, Not Walls." There are many, many more messages and policy actions having to do with domestic and international affairs. The church early on opposed the war in Iraq.

These public pronouncements are supplemented generously by the ELCA Presiding Bishop, who comments on a large number of public issues, both international and domestic. He calls for implementation of the Peace, Not Walls strategy. He laments the snows melting on Kilimanjaro and calls for a dramatic anti-global warming strategy that would "end our dependence on oil." (Not diminish such dependence, but end it!) After the election of 2008, he suggested a program to the new President — alternative energy to establish a new green economy, reengagement with the peace process for Israel and the Palestinians, U.S. funding of the Millennium Goals, a robust diplomatic effort to "restore U.S. credibility abroad" — that resembles not only President Obama's campaign emphases, but also those of the Democratic Party.

Admittedly, 95 percent of the laypersons of the ELCA do not have a clue about these utterances; perhaps a few more clergy know about them. But if the laity suddenly became aware of these, a goodly portion would be very irritated, if not offended, because at least half of the Lutheran laity are conservative. They would wonder how such a straight line was drawn from core Christian principles to liberal political policies. They would suspect that the "intervening factors" we talked about in Chapter Four were far more influential in the shaping of the statements than the core convictions themselves. Or, at the very least, they would see alternative ways of reaching the goals that the liberal policies were aiming at. They would wonder about all this, and they would be right to wonder.

This promiscuity in issuing statements dramatically reduces the moral credibility of the liberal Protestant churches, many of which are even busier than the ELCA. They are following their ecumenical agencies — the World and National Council of Churches — in squandering their capacity to make a genuine prophetic witness. They simply are too identified with partisan political options — and therefore too predictable — to have the needed distance from all that to be genuinely prophetic.

In earlier decades the Catholic Bishops of America issued more influential statements on major issues, but they too tended to identify too easily with liberal politics. In recent years their moral capital has been sharply eroded by sexual misconduct scandals. The exception to this general Catholic decline seems to be the various encyclicals and letters offered by the last two Popes — John Paul II and now Benedict XVI — whose moral exhortations are headlined in the media and taken seriously by many sectors of society. They are treated far more seriously than any of the Protestant efforts.

Meanwhile the evangelical churches seem to have learned how to play the same political game as their liberal Protestant counterparts. They want to influence their own people and the public sector with many pronouncements. For example, *The Ethics & Religious Liberty Commission* of the Southern Baptists resists many of the policies that the Lutherans commend. They also agitate on social issues — abortion, pornography, the legal protection of traditional marriage — that the liberal Protestant denominations will not address. The National Association of Evangelicals' Office of Governmental Affairs takes a more modest path, but yet tends to come down on the opposite side of the liberal Protestant statements. These agencies tend to represent more accurately the public policy convictions of their laity than do the liberal Protestant churches and therefore exert more influence in church and society. Indeed, this growing influence is precisely what has produced the explosion of books arguing for what we called earlier "selective separationism." The nervous authors of these books rarely worry about the liberal Protestant identification with progressive causes, but frantically ring the alarm about conservative Protestant support for conservative causes.

Our argument is that all churches and their leaders ought to be far more circumspect in their efforts to affect the political realm through direct influence. There is certainly an obligation to carry on a prophetic ministry when that is strongly called for, but those cases are far fewer than is assumed by those churches. We have also suggested ways to be prophetic that do not assume that churches and their leaders have special competence in the realm of public policy, thus usurping the role of the Christian laity in that calling. We tend to agree with C. S. Lewis that "[t]he application of Christian principles, say, to trade unionism or education, must come from Christian unionists and Christian schoolmasters: just as Christian literature comes from Christian novelists and dramatists — not from the bench of bishops getting together and trying to write plays and novels in their spare time" (*Mere Christianity*, p. 75).

Yet, there are times and places when direct influence is called for. We have enumerated some of them above — by saying "no," by non-compliance in church life, by dramatically calling attention to injustice or neglect, and by pioneering a Christian approach to social challenges in the life of churches themselves. And there is room for well-crafted social statements if they are characterized by the following guidelines: 1) They should be relatively infrequent. The church should only speak when it has something special to say from its own religious resources. It should speak only when it has to, otherwise it should remain quiet. 2) Such statements should engage in serious preparation, careful consideration, widespread critique and revision, and should reflect a strong theological and ethical consensus. Such requirements will dictate that there will be fewer of them than there are. 3) Church social statements ought clearly to distinguish different circles or levels of authority — high authority and near unanimity on core religious convictions, strong authority for long-held moral and social teachings of the church, less authority for how the contemporary church assesses the issues before it and applies core principles to those issues, and much latitude about how Christians come down on particular policies. These distinctions will diminish the tendency to engage in "straight-line thinking." 4) Church social statements should observe the means/ends distinction. Many Christians agree on the general goals to which Christian convictions point, but disagree very strongly on the means to achieve them. As we pointed out earlier, those differences often hinge on Christians drawing on different aspects of the Christian intellectual and moral tradition. A wise approach to church social statements would point out a number of ways that important goals might be achieved, lift up critical reflections on each way, and allow laypeople to make up their minds. Such an approach fits well with what we earlier called "the ethics of conscience."

In conclusion, there is certainly room for the direct influence of the church[2] if it is handled wisely. There are indeed times

---

2. Let us be clear here that I am speaking about the church as an institution, not about its laypeople or about voluntary associations spawned by the church. They have great latitude to argue and act for a wide variety of partisan perspectives and policies. Let a thousand flowers bloom in those cases. They are not entrusted with the proclamation of the gospel for all sinners in the way that churches are. I believe it is a sign of health when churches firmly hold and share their core convictions but stimulate a wide variety of responses to those convictions.

when the church must speak out with an impassioned "no," times when it must resist evil, and times when it must argue the case for policies that closely track or clearly oppose its deepest convictions. But those times are not nearly as frequent as our American churches aver. It would be far better to speak less often on fewer issues but with more prophetic power.

### Direct and Intentional Action — the Church with Power

The final way of relating church and politics is highly controversial and risky for both church and society. That is *direct and intentional action.* It is direct because the church becomes an institutional actor in society. It is intentional in that the church intends to support particular policies or move society in certain directions. Further, and here is the rub, the church uses *power* to realize its intentions. It no longer relies solely on the persuasiveness of argument or example; it commits its funds, political weight, and people-power to pressure relevant decision-makers to move toward a specific policy objective. It exerts coercive power. There are many examples of this mode of relating church to political life, many of them used as egregious examples of religion becoming violent and repressive. For example, when Constantine made Christianity the religion of the realm, church and state began to partner in imposing imperial and ecclesial objectives on various populations. It was difficult to tell where the power of the state ended and the power of the church began. Instead of the church suffering under empire, it became part of empire. So the church was able to use the coercive power of the state to suppress pagan religions and their practices. The Crusades were part of an effort militarily and politically to recapture the Holy Land that had been lost to Muslim power.

In many instances, the church "evangelized" behind the

power of the state. Whole tribes of pagans became Christians under kings who held the Bible in one hand and a sword in the other. In the Middle Ages the Popes became deeply involved in coercive power. The Reformers protested this churchly involvement in power, claiming that such involvement distorted the mission of the church and corrupted both the church and the political realm. Indeed, the Roman Church used the power of the state to stamp out the Protestants' efforts at reform. In turn, Protestants used political power to protect themselves but also to extend their hegemony. The Catholic tendency to use its own and the state's coercive power to further its own purposes lasted until very recently. Now, however, the Catholic Church has in principle abjured its prerogative to use coercive power. It tends now to rely on the power of persuasion, partly because it has little direct political power. One could argue that the history of the West is one long lesson about the inadvisability of the church getting too directly involved in political power. While Christendom was in many ways the admirable product of such closeness to power, it is good for the church that that era is past. Christendom is unlikely to return.

Such is not the case with Islam's relation to political power, however. The rise of militant Islam has brought a strong drive for Muslim religious authorities to exert coercive power in both religious and political life. The move toward Sharia (the religious law spelled out in the Koran) in many Muslim countries means the direct involvement of organized Islam in political power. Muslim militancy has even intimidated European "Christian" countries into ceding some direct political power to Muslim religious authorities in those countries.

Examples of the churches' involvement in direct power are much fewer and milder in the contemporary democratic West, contrary to what the "separationists" claim are the intentions of conservative churches. Even among American fundamentalist churches and other members of the so-called "Religious Right," there are very few who believe the church should actually wield power directly. It is a horribly distorting charge that equates the dangers of American fundamentalism with that of Islamic. Churches at all points along the religious spectrum recognize the riskiness of this direct involvement in power. Most of the direct involvement comes from voluntary associations that are independent of the churches, yet are staffed and supported by Christians. For example, the boycotts declared by the American Family Association cause less turbulence in the church simply because the AFA is not the church, but rather a freestanding Christian voluntary association. The direct involvement of these groups in political or economic power is at the same time the indirect involvement of the church itself.

Further, given the vastness and variety of American power centers, it is quite a stretch to worry overmuch about those churches "taking over." It is highly unlikely that our society can be seriously swayed or harmed by churches becoming involved directly in political power. However, the damage to churches when they opt for this mode of relation to politics is much more serious.

Yet, there are churches that risk such involvement. A good domestic example of direct action comes from the community organization movement, particularly those influenced by that great activist, Saul Alinsky. Community organizations associated with his Industrial Areas Foundation generally require that churches as institutions, not simply as Christian individuals, join the community organization. The churches have to commit money, leadership, and the "troops" to its operations. The community organization, moreover, frequently uses "conflict methods" in its engagement with the powers that be. That involves dramatic protests and symbolic actions, boycotts, civil disobedience, divestment of funds, picketing of businesses, and many other contentious efforts. These requirements and methods are intended to be coercive and present churches with difficult choices concerning their direct participation in power. Many local parishes have split over those choices while denominations have anguished about the propriety of such involvement.

An ongoing controversy over direct action follows from many churches' engagement in "advocacy." This is a mild form of direct action, yet one that illustrates its ambiguities. Churches maintain offices of governmental affairs in Washington and in state capitals. They advocate for particular policies, some that correspond with the churches' statements on social issues, about which I wrote above. In the case of "advocacy," however, the churches' governmental affairs offices go beyond the persuasive influence of social statements, such as they might be. The offices want members of the churches to contact their representatives in sufficient numbers to pressure them to vote for the preferred policies. There are scores and scores of these initiatives on the part of churches with advocacy offices, some of them having little relation to the formal statements of the churches, but much to do with the political predilections of the advocates themselves. (I receive several "alerts" per week from our church's advocacy office to notify my Senator or Representative about this or that policy, which I am often against.) And, sadly, the preferred policies of the mainline Protestant churches are liberal while the preferred policies of the conservative churches are conservative. Thus, one begins to suspect an unfortunate "fusion" of religion and politics is going on.

Some direct actions of the churches are not so mild. For example, the Presbyterian Church USA has had a continuing effort by its agencies to get the church to divest from corporations doing business in Israel, particularly those having anything to do with Israeli military activities. This has brought forth huge protests from Presbyterians as well as sharp criticism from others outside the church, particularly Jewish individuals and organizations. This example echoes the earlier efforts of many churches to divest from companies that did business in Apartheid South Africa. Those efforts brought rancorous divisiveness to the churches. Currently, churches with "social responsibility" offices also badger businesses to adopt the preferred policies of the churches. These efforts usually "fly under the radar" and therefore are not as controversial as the more public campaigns to divest.

By and large, this direct-action approach to politics should be avoided, not so much for fear of injury to society but for what it can do to the church. It too easily makes the church into a partisan society that tends to run roughshod over the legitimate political opinions of too many people in the church. It infuriates people who have a different perspective on debatable public policies.

Further, it involves the church in a confusion of functions. Secular authorities and agencies are the appropriate wielders of power in society. Churches are quintessentially themselves when they rely on the power of the Word, and on their example, not on worldly might.

Even more seriously, direct action threatens to instrumentalize and secularize the sacred symbols of the church in pursuit of very secular, partisan agendas. The church loses its needed distance from all political action; its claim to point to transcendence collapses if it draws too close to a program of political action. Consequently, it has a more difficult time proclaiming a universal gospel to all sinners regardless of what side of the political fence they are on. Certainly this has been a tendency of all churches too closely allied to political authority and too deeply involved in political power. (Fortunately, most local parishes do not get this close to political programs and therefore do not make the mistakes I have just enumerated. However, alert laypeople who watch the actions of the national church are often put off by its politicization.)

Generally speaking, when direct action is called for, it is much better for the church to let that be carried on by laity in their worldly roles or by voluntary associations that are distinct from the church. Dietrich Bonhoeffer had an astute intuition when he insisted that the assassination plot on Hitler in which he was involved — what a form of direct action! — be carried out by an informal group of Christians, not by the church itself.

In spite of all these reservations, however, there are occasions when direct action is a necessary way of proceeding. There may be compelling reasons for the church to get involved directly in the application of power. One of them might be that the church may responsibly get directly engaged when there are no other organizations capable of taking decisive action in a chaotic or repressive society. A good argument could be made that the church responsibly engaged in serious power-play during the chaotic fall of the Roman Empire. One could also make a good case that the Polish Catholic Church's direct support of the Solidarity movement during the time of Soviet oppression was such an exceptional case. In that situation the church was the only relatively free and strong organization in a society under totalitarian rule. Likewise, the Catholic Church was probably wise in helping the Filipinos support a democrat for President rather than a corrupt authoritarian, just as it is perhaps necessary currently for the churches of Zimbabwe to support political alternatives to Mugabe.

But these are exceptional cases, and it is wise for the church to withdraw from direct political engagement once the crisis is over. In most cases the church quickly withdraws from this sort of action, recognizing the dangers to its life and mission involved in such direct enmeshment.

These, then, are the four ways that organized religion practically connects with the political order, running from the decidedly non-controversial to the most controversial and risky. If the church is really the church, the first and second types are the most fundamental and effective ways that it affects the political process. In a relatively just, pluralistic, and stable society, the first three modes should predominate. Nevertheless, there are instances of injustice in this society and in the world when the church might responsibly engage in direct action. But it should do so with full awareness that what it is doing ought to be temporary and infrequent.

## Conclusion

As we conclude our reflections on bad and good ways that people think about religion and politics, it is fitting to make a few summary comments. First, because of the nature of serious religion, it cannot be separated from politics. Furthermore, the First Amendment gives robust rights to religious persons and institutions to express publicly the political judgments and actions that are motivated by and flow from religious convictions. There can be no complete or even partial separation between religion and politics. The "wall of separation" is impossible, even at the institutional level.

Likewise, there is grave danger to religion in fusing religion and politics. Such fusion, which is almost always unintentional, has the devastating effect of reducing the transcendent claims of religion to partisan politics. That severely damages the church and its mission. The fusion of religion and society is less of a problem for American society because of its profusion of centers of power, most of which are not religious in character. But such fusion does inject a harshness and bitterness into political fights that are better left by the wayside. Politics are full of enough conflict without investing them with full religious legitimation.

Yet, we argued that central religious convictions are definitely related to politics, but that relationship is rarely character-ized by a straight line from central convictions to public policy. There are many steps in moving from core theological convic-tions to public policy, and well-intentioned and well-informed Christians often part company with each step. And there are many facets of the Christian moral and intellectual tradition upon which persons of differing political persuasions draw. There may indeed be a straight line from the core to the public policy in God's unerring mind, but we sinful and finite human beings cannot enjoy such certainty. We can only grope for the best connections we can discover.

There are some political policies that may follow a straighter line from core to public policy than others. We argued that three of them might be such: policies that protect religious freedom and the free exercise of religion; policies that protect the most vulnerable of human lives; and a generous safety net for those in our society who clearly cannot make their way in the society. Even those straighter lines are not all that straight when we come to the formulation of public policy, which is fraught with all sorts of compromises and unintended effects.

Such toleration of different public policy choices is not un-limited, however. There are times when societies go in wicked di-rections to which the church must say "no" as clearly as possible, and resist with all its spiritual weapons. May God grant that we are spared such challenges.

Finally, we have argued that the church can affect political life most profoundly in indirect ways — through the witness of fully formed Christian disciples in their callings and through the work of independent voluntary associations spawned by the church. But we have left room for direct influence — persuasive statements by the church to the society — and even for direct ac-tion in times of crisis. Religion and politics must be rightly con-nected for the good of both.

113

# Index